THE TREE AT THE CENTER OF THE WORLD

THE TREE AT THE

A Story of the California Missions

CENTER OF THE WORLD

BY BRUCE WALTER BARTON

Design and photography by the author

ROSS-ERIKSON PUBLISHERS, INC. SANTA BARBARA

SIR HARRY DOWNIE, K.S.G.
The Architect of Restoration

Printed in the United States of America.

Library of Congress Cataloging in Publication Data

Barton, Bruce Walter, 1935-
    The tree at the center of the world.

    Bibliography: p.
    Includes index.
    1. Missions—California—History. 2. Missions,
Spanish. 3. Spaniards in California—History.
4. Indians of North America—California—Missions.
5. California—History—To 1846. I. Title.
F864.B25   266'.2'794   79-26434
ISBN 0-915520-30-3
ISBN 0-915520-29-X pbk.

ROSS-ERIKSON PUBLISHERS, INC., 629 State Street,
Santa Barbara, CA   93101

Introduction

The Spanish Missions of California's EL CAMINO REAL, as the many other Spanish sites in the "New World," are not just perishable historical monuments, residues of a complete past. These Missions, rather, are living voices each of which speaks with its own particular eloquence of the presence within North America of a cultural heritage that is still alive and with us. This is a heritage of values and beliefs, of saints and sinners, of Sword and Cross, of unique art forms speaking of and from *two* worlds, of a unique and creative religious presence, and above all of *encounter* of this presence with those indigenous native peoples who probably were more numerous in California than in any other area of North America. The roots of this encounter between peoples of vastly contrasting yet mutually rich cultures were planted and tended during some three centuries of Spanish presence in North America; a presence that commenced twenty-two years before the pilgrims landed at Plymouth Rock, ten years before French Quebec, and nine years before the English Jamestown. Whether we accept these earliest Spanish roots or not, they are nevertheless entwined in living manner within the many threads which constitute the fabric of what America is.

Documenting, illuminating, and commenting on this Spanish presence in the "New World," is a wealth of literature: historical, scholarly, anthropological, and romantic. And inevitably, there are also those records and commentaries which, through commission and omission, and out of bias and prejudice, falsify the true nature of this Spanish presence and mission in North America. Many questions and problems, therefore, remain to be addressed both with human understanding and with that critical sense which any problematic historical epoch demands. If the mood of America's present moment seeks to lay hold of roots which tell of origin, which speak of the sense and meaning of place, and of *who* we are in time and place, pointing us perhaps towards new and positive alternatives, then the reality of some three centuries of Spanish presence is not inconsequential. Any new, imaginative, and careful study of the multiple dimensions of this presence is therefore to be applauded. And especially to be applauded is that human warmth of understanding which this present work by Bruce Walter Barton represents.

A source of the wide-spread and continuing misrepresentations of Spain's role in the colonizing of large areas of North America may in part be laid to those earlier American texts whose origin and center of distribution tended to be the New England of Protestant reformation persuasion. Indeed, this was an era insisting not only on the separation of Church and State, but even on the impossible separation of ecclesiastical and secular history! For the greatest threat of Spain to the New Republic was precisely the presence of pre-reformation Catholic-European, religious, social, legal, political, and cultural elements. If these Catholic presences were unacceptable, not to say dangerous, to that formative period of America, nevertheless, if a position of greater temporal and ideological distance be taken, it may at the least be said that the Spanish presence is unique and potentially positive. This is a positive presence at least in the sense that it alone provided America with a direct historical link to pre-reformation Europe, and thus back to Mediaeval Europe which, from one point of view, may be said to represent the flowering of a truly Christian civilization. An especially vital thread of this intensely religio-centered civilization carried on into America particularly through the great religious Orders, notably the Franciscans, whose dedicated friars led sacramental lives in establishing the Missions of the Southwest and later those of California's EL CAMINO REAL.

The remarkable quality of person of the friars of the Franciscan Order, as distinguished from the supporting military of the Presidio, certainly helps to explain what seems to have been their effective persuasion over no small number of the indigenous native peoples. It is indeed this encounter of the Catholic religion with the native tribes that presents moments of history which are particularly unique to world history; and yet, it is the critical treatment of the real nature of this interface that is almost totally lacking in the literature. Statistical entries on numbers of converts, for example, tell us nothing of the quality of inner experience for the person in this encounter between Christianity, a historical religion essentially Mediaeval in form and message, and those native non-historical "primitive" religious traditions whose rich origins lie in a primordial antiquity. How are we to understand that seeming instant willingness, at least as the Christian documents attest, of native persons to live and work within what must have been very alien structures and strictures of the Mission communities? For conversion to the western Christian mind tends to connote a clear either-or choice, thus the necessity for near immediate transformation of the deepest realities of the soul, as well as near abandonment of many of those native cultural patterns deeply integrated within the totality of their lives and life-ways. Such structures, further, are supported and born by the native languages each of which is richly specific to the people's particular cultural values and world views.

Obviously there were reciprocal "trade-offs" which transpired as the Church itself was inevitably touched by a range of native artistic, cultural, and ceremonial forms and forces, just as the native cultures also were bent to accommodate selective Christian elements. Certainly the padres wisely did not insist on too rapid a transition, for they learned and supported the use of native languages, or at least until the Crown declared otherwise, and they did tolerate continuance of many of the peoples' ancient customs. But again, out of this encounter was there more than tolerance? That is, to what extent and depth did the Padres actually seek to uncover and understand beliefs and sacred lore of the Native Americans' own religious traditions? Historical records and subsequent commentary remain too mute on this question.

Could it be correct to suggest that in this encounter the native peoples were in fact learning to accommodate themselves to two cultures without completely rejecting either? This facility for flexibility, for learning to cope with the apparent inevitability of the moment, is certainly a pervasive phenomenon obtaining among probably all native peoples to this day. Whether innate or learned, this trait has allowed the people to survive.

In addressing these questions, as must be done in studies still to be accomplished, it may be instructive to compare and contrast the apparent success of the California Missions to the less successful record of the earlier Franciscan Missions of the American Southwest. It is here too simplistic a criteria to distinguish a Mission's success or failure on the basis of individual personalities, a Junipero Serra for example, or a Father Kino? Or, is the degree of people's nomadic, semi-nomadic, or sedentary life a determinant? It would certainly seem obvious that a nomadic people would have the greater difficulty in adjusting to the sedentary structures of Mission or pueblo. In California there were both sedentary and semi-nomadic groups, and indeed it was particularly the latter group who offered on occasion great resistance to all missionizing attempts, as did the nomadic Comanches and Athabaskans of the Southwest. And yet in the Southwest the sedentary peoples of the eastern and western "Pueblos" underwent successive and successful rebellions to both Sword and Cross, albeit eventually having no choice but to develop means for appearing to conform while guarding their own sacred lore and calendric ceremonies underground — a pattern continuing to this day as the people are under great pressures for change issuing from many forces other than the Church. The final answer to all these questions might be that, transcending personalities and cultural variations, in Its own mysterious manner the Spirit moves where and as It wills and no socio-cultural, ethnographic or geographic factors can be fixed as ultimate determinants.

Other questions rising from comparisons are presented in the relative success of the Catholic Padres in the apparent conversions of native Americans in contrast to the Protestant endeavors in areas not under the military control of the Catholic Spanish or French. Certainly the historical Protestant vision of the basic nature of the "native savage" does not seem to have been as generous or enlightened as that of the Spanish Catholic. Although proclamations may only express ideal theory and not live reality, nevertheless the 1537 Papal Bull, SUBLIMIS DEUS, of Paul III may be relevant to our question:

> "The said Indians and all other people who may be discovered by Christians, are by no means to be deprived of their liberty or the possession of their property, even though they may be outside of the faith of Jesus Christ."

One suggestive factor clarifying possibly the apparent relative missionizing success of the Catholic Church over that of the Protestant sects, might be found in the fact that the depth, richness, and indeed great complexity of the Native American's own religious beliefs, supporting rites and sacred forms, led to an ease in their understanding of, and thus possible transition to, that parallel richness of Catholic doctrine, practice, and formal sacred expressions. The relative simplicity of many Protestant ecclestical doctrines and forms may not have been as attractive to those native peoples who generally had great respect and appreciation for formal ceremonial behaviour, and who affirmed the sacred through a rich body of lore integrated into the totality of their lifeways. It would indeed be difficult in native cultures to find any area of the peoples' lives which did not relate to a sacred perspective.

In creative and comprehensive manner, and with a simple forceful style reminiscent of a Mission fresco, Bruce Walter Barton has in this volume contributed, with great warmth of intention, a wealth of materials for our understanding and evaluation of the philosophical perspectives and historical problems sampled in the very general introductory paragraphs above. Through his splendid photographs and a rich array of historical facts, and with many very human anecdotes, we are led on a pilgrimage from the 13th century founding of the Franciscan Order through the some 21 Missions of the Royal EL CAMINO REAL. This is the first work on the Missions to give in such fair and comprehensive manner attention to the ethnographic details of those native peoples for whom and by whom the Missions were essentially established. In this pilgrimage Professor Barton has taken a welcome and objective middle course, neither contrasting pious friars of a civilized world with ignorant uncivilized savages, nor romanticizing on noble Indians destroyed by ruthless representatives of Church and Crown. Further, the journey has been undertaken with that warmth and respect which can only be accomplished by one who has traveled the *Way* through a period of many years. Above all, he has been personally touched by what he has seen.

Both Christian and native belief, ritual, and iconographic forms are here elevated and illuminated through suggestive and often subtle parallels occuring between two otherwise very disparate traditions: the Tree at the Center of the World, the Language of Sacred Dance and Song, the sacramental feast, the modes and nature of communion and community. And as the journey of both

Mission and the Native American speak of the cycle of life, through birth, growth, death and new life, we are here exposed to universal themes which cannot be the exclusive province of any one people or of one religious tradition exclusively.

If we are mystified by those Coyote tracks which wander at random through the text, it is to remind us through a native means that essentially we are dealing here not just with an account of a particular history, but of History, and encounter beyond history, wherein the total gamut of human proclivities and activities, from the exalted to the most base and ridiculous, are indeed those realities of the human condition. Coyote tracks may wander and have no end, but the Tree always is at the center of the world.

Joseph Epes Brown
Author, *The Sacred Pipe*

Overleaf:
Infant Jesus

INFANT JESUS
CIRCA 1900

Introduction   VII
THE CALIFORNIA MISSIONS   1

The Missions of Francis   7
The Continent of One Thousand Tribes   13
The People   23

THE TREE AT THE CENTER
OF THE WORLD   35

A TREE TAKES ROOT:
Mission San Diego de Alcala   43

PERSONAGES AT THE TREE:
Mission San Carlos Borromeo de Carmelo   53

THE TRADE-OFF BEGINS:
Mission San Antonio de Padua   61

A TREE AT THE CROSSROADS:
Mission San Gabriel Arcangel   69

EXTERNAL INFLUENCES:
Mission San Luis Obispo de Tolosa   77

THE TREE AS SYMBOL:
Mission San Francisco de Asis (Dolores)   85

THE SACRED DANCE   95

SILENT VESTIGES OF THE DANCE:
Mission San Juan Capistrano   109

THE DANCE OF THE CHURCH:
Mission Santa Clara de Asis   119

THE COVENANT AND THE CANOE:
Mission San Buenaventura   129

THE DANCE OF SOLITUDE:
Mission Santa Barbara   137

TOWARD A CHRISTIAN EDUCATION:
Mission La Purisima Concepcion   149

THE SACRED FEAST   159

THE FEAST OF FOOLS:
Mission Santa Cruz   165

A COMMUNITY IN RETREAT:
Mission Nuestra Senora de la Soledad   173

POVERTY, PROSPERITY AND THE PARADOX:
Mission San Jose   181

THE HEADY ROSE AND HARDY WINE:
Mission San Juan Bautista   191

AGONY AND ABUNDANCE:
Mission San Miguel Arcangel   203

THE PLAINSONG

THE PLAINSONG 219

OUR LADY AND HER CONSORT:
Mission San Fernando Rey de Espana 231

FATHER PEYRI'S SONG:
Mission San Luis Rey de Francia 243

A MATTER OF JUDGMENT:
Mission Santa Ines 257

A QUESTION OF PRIDE:
Mission San Rafael Arcangel 265

AT THE EDGE OF THE END:
Mission San Francisco de Solano 277

A LONG STILLNESS:
The Period of Secularization 289

REBIRTH AND RESTORATION:
Sir Harry Downie, Architect 297

Acknowledgment 307
Appendix 310
List of Illustrations 313
Selected Bibliography and Additional Readings 315
Index of People and Places 318

THE
California
Missions

- 21 SAN FRANCISCO DE SOLANO
- 20 SAN RAFAEL ARCANGEL
- 6 SAN FRANCISCO DE ASIS
- 14 SAN JOSE
- 8 SANTA CLARA
- 12 SANTA CRUZ
- 15 SAN JUAN BAUTISTA
- 2 SAN CARLOS BORROMEO DE CARMELO
- 13 NUESTRA SENORA DE LA SOLEDAD
- 3 SAN ANTONIO DE PADUA
- 16 SAN MIGUEL ARCANGEL
- 5 SAN LUIS OBISPO DE TOLOSA
- 11 LA PURISIMA CONCEPCION
- 19 SANTA INES
- 10 SANTA BARBARA
- 9 SAN BUENAVENTURA
- 17 SAN FERNANDO REY DE ESPANA
- 4 SAN GABRIEL ARCANGEL
- 7 SAN JUAN CAPISTRANO
- 18a SAN ANTONIO DE PALA
- 18 SAN LUIS REY DE FRANCIA
- 1 SAN DIEGO DE ALCALA

The story of the California missions is a story of community. As the tale unfolds, one finds two ancient and powerful traditions at work, for it was in mission life that Native America confronted Roman Catholic Spain. In these communities a trade-off occurred in which the natives gave new expression to Catholicism, and Catholicism, in turn, had significant impact upon the indigenous Americans. Although the exchange was sometimes imperceptible, at other times forceful and abrupt, in California both traditions came to expression anew.

A glance at a California map during the mission period — the years between 1769 and 1835 — indicates that the missions, together with the *asistencias* (or satellite units), dotted either side of El Camino Real like so many

The
California
Missions

wildflowers. However, only twenty-one facilities were complete, self-sufficient Christian communities with full mission status. Within each, dedicated Franciscan priests, or "padres," provided leadership and guidance, while inspiration was furnished by appropriate Roman Catholic saints in whose custody the facilities were placed and after whom they were named. Perhaps it is more than mere coincidence that there often exists a unique connection between the name of a given mission and the stories and events that surround it.

The Franciscan Missions formed a chain of independent, yet spiritually united communities that followed the general contour of the coastline. The Camino Real — the famous trail which linked them — stretched from San Diego in the south to Sonoma in the north, and though the twenty-one missions were not constructed at perfectly regular intervals along this road, a foot traveler could leave one community in the early hours of the morning and with relative ease arrive under the protection of the next mission before nightfall.

These twenty-one facilities held much in common, despite the fact that the major industries or trades may have varied somewhat from mission to mission. In addition to the church, each facility included a library, kitchen and smithy, storerooms, stables and living quarters, as well as shops for making soap and candles and facilities for spinning, weaving, and woodworking. There was also a tannery which, because of its objectionable odor, was normally relegated to the greatest safe distance. Most mission buildings followed a

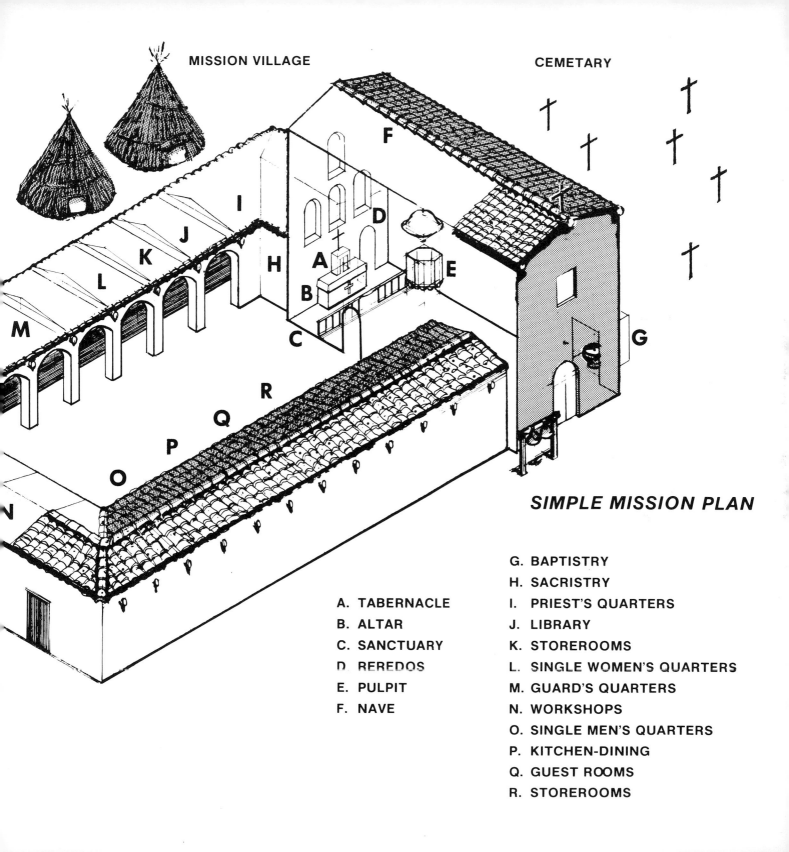

MISSION VILLAGE

CEMETARY

F

I

J

K

L

M

N

O

P

Q

R

H

A

B

C

D

E

G

SIMPLE MISSION PLAN

A. TABERNACLE

B. ALTAR

C. SANCTUARY

D. REREDOS

E. PULPIT

F. NAVE

G. BAPTISTRY

H. SACRISTY

I. PRIEST'S QUARTERS

J. LIBRARY

K. STOREROOMS

L. SINGLE WOMEN'S QUARTERS

M. GUARD'S QUARTERS

N. WORKSHOPS

O. SINGLE MEN'S QUARTERS

P. KITCHEN-DINING

Q. GUEST ROOMS

R. STOREROOMS

quadrangle design and were protected by a palisade.

The Native American converts who peopled these facilities also had much in common. They shared a liturgical life and engaged in similar crafts and trades, kept cattle, and tended gardens on the mission grounds. They made wine and brandy; they baked bread.

The Missions
Today

Presently, the twenty-one missions can be found in a variety of environments — on a remote army base, at the heart of a university, in an urban area, or in communities that appear otherwise almost without life. All are now much reduced in size, and exist in various states of reconstruction. Some are even without their former grace — a product of overmodernization or overindulgence — but the majority retain the power and authority befitting a proper Roman Catholic church.

The Mission
Story

In gathering information about these old missions, and in talking to those who have stories about them, it is found that while most of the events reported are faithful to historical detail, many are borrowed from other times and other places; and some are in fact pure fabrications. Nonetheless, each story has its purpose — contributing something useful, something valuable, making the tale of each mission more "truly" true than a mere collection of facts could. Thus, as fact and fancy become gently blurred, the entire mission event can best be appreciated as a special kind of American folklore, similar to the Native American fables known as *Coyote Tales.*

4 Such myths present the complexity of factors at work in life;

they reveal penetrating truths; they provide a mirror in which to see ourselves and our humanity.

Today, the California missions are often considered merely old curiosities, no more than footnotes to the story of great world traditions. But no matter how subtle or vigorous their contribution may have been in the past, the tradition of the spirit is ongoing and present among them. As part of California's living history, they are the enduring remnants of a much larger cloth.

————————

The Missions of Francis:

The Franciscans were men charged to serve both the body and the soul, a role for which their humble dispositions and rigorous training had thoroughly prepared them. They were members of the Order of Friars Minor, which, though founded as a mendicant order — a group committed to begging for sustenance — nonetheless boasts within its ranks of an

Opposite page:
St. Francis of Assisi

7

impressive list of scholars and theologians including Roger Bacon, Duns Scotus, and St. Bonaventure.

St. Francis
of Assisi

The Order continues to honor the name of its famous founder and guide, St. Francis of Assisi. Francis was born in Assisi, a walled town in the Italian province of Umbria, in approximately 1182. At birth he was named John, but his father, a merchant in fabrics and a man of considerable means, soon nicknamed him *Francesco* — "the Frenchman" — the name by which he came to be known.

We know that in his youth Francis had not been well-educated, and evidence suggests that he was quixotic and of no more than average intelligence. The gifts which gave him his enduring qualities were instead faith, courage, and a special kind of personal magnetism. Like the other young men of his day, Francis in his early years was influenced by the material pleasures of life, such as fashionable clothing, good spirits, and dancing. He was popular with his friends and associates, and generally considered something of a "sport."

Francis'
Visions

However, one day while with his friends he was struck speechless by a "visitation," and he afterwards told them that he had taken a bride "nobler, richer, and fairer than you have ever seen." Thereafter, he became introspective, regularly engaging in meditation and prayer, and began to take an interest in the well-being of those more unfortunate than he.

Throughout his life Francis continued to have visions, the details of which he often tended to take too literally, at the expense of the symbolic or metaphorical interpretation. Once, while praying before a painted figure of Christ in the nearby chapel of San Damiano, Francis experienced such a vision: in it he was instructed to "go forward and repair the Church." In his usual fashion, young Francis assigned the most obvious significance to the event and immediately made plans to rebuild the tiny chapel in which he stood. Unhappily, as part of his fund-raising scheme he sold a load of his father's merchandise — as well as the horse that carried it!

The Mission
of
Francis

Fully anticipating the fury of the merchant, San Damiano's resident priest refused the money Francis offered. His perceptions were of course quite correct — the merchant was enraged. Francis himself reacted by hiding out among the surrounding hills. It was not long afterwards that he was summoned to an audience at the palace of the bishop where, with a dramatic gesture, he abruptly disavowed worldly goods and took up the rags of a beggar.

After his public vow of poverty, Francis left Assisi and traveled north. In 1206 he experienced another vision — one that secured his future and made clear the arduous career that lay before him. It was during a Mass that the insight came: as Francis prayed he was instructed to conduct his life, without compromise, after the model of Jesus. With this sense of "mission" visited upon him, the twenty-five year old youth donned a long grey robe of coarse material and secured it with a piece of rope. Thus was born the Order of Friars Minor — the Franciscans.

The
Franciscans

9

The remainder of Francis's years were spent fulfilling his vision — traveling from community to community, building, teaching, healing, cleaning. Among his early tasks Francis ministered to lepers and restored ruined churches. ("Go forward and repair the church!") He supported himself by begging — much to the horror of his disapproving family — sometimes obtaining food, but just as often being driven away or assaulted with stones. Despite setbacks, however, Francis continued with his mission. He had a truly charismatic personality, and he preached in the streets, in public places, and anywhere at all where he might find a listener. It is even reported that Francis, who particularly enjoyed the companionship of birds, had often been seen preaching to them!

The life-style of St. Francis proved sufficiently compelling to attract first one, then several young men, then more, to the extent that by 1209 the citizens of Assisi expressed alarm at the number of young men who were giving away their worldly goods and joining Francis. They feared that the whole generation would turn to begging for subsistence and would soon be at their door. The group was constantly half naked and near starvation. People often fled from them believing them to be not quite human. Yet Francis's preachings and attacks on social injustice continued to draw followers. His group divided itself into pairs and went throughout the countryside carrying the message of the Gospels. In 1210 they reunited at Assisi, and as Francis had given them all permission to add recruits, they now constituted a religious community.

The young friars filled their days with manual labor and preaching. New recruits were added throughout 1211 and the breadth of their gifts was enhanced as they were joined by men of diverse background and training. In 1212 the community acquired a permanent residence in northern Italy.

The Order of Friars Minor became international in reputation and influence, and by 1276 their numbers had swelled to two hundred thousand. These early Franciscans, choosing to associate themselves with victims of misfortune by teaching and tending the sick and the poor, were the precursors of the Franciscans who in later years established themselves in Mexico and the United States.

The Continent of One Thousand Tribes:

The continents that have come to be called North and South America, naively referred to by Eureopeans as the "New World," were indeed not that at all, having been populated long before the time of St. Francis. There is even evidence to suggest that the western coasts of what are now Mexico and California were visited on occasion, if not frequently, by the Chinese. Such trips are not at all unlikely, given the nature of prevailing ocean currents, and perhaps time will prove this influence to have been much greater than is presently obvious. The Japanese, too, had ample opportunity to establish an Oriental control over these lands, although their reasons for refraining may have had more to do with politics than geography.

So it appears inevitable that some nation would come to turn the world upside down for the indigenous people living in small villages along the coast. That nation was the Spanish, who were the first permanent intruders into the "Continent of 1000 Tribes," and whose military arm freely cut and gouged its way into American history.

Following the incursion into the continent by Christopher Columbus, the Spanish occupation began in the West Indies and later Panama. Then, in 1519 Hernando Cortez and a small army arrived at Vera Cruz, and by 1521 this famous explorer had headquartered himself in Mexico City. A year later he crossed the continent and settled at Zacatula, from where he led sea expeditions northward along the western coast.

Although Cortez was himself a subject of the King of Spain, the great distance from his homeland initially permitted him unusual authority. He was at once chief justice, captain-general, and governor of New Spain. For years he exercised unrestrained power.

Cortez was a remarkable man — certainly a very tenacious

one — as the obstacles to his northward exploration of the coast were almost without limit. For one, he had no ships, nor anyone trained to build them. Yet under this direction and in the most adverse of circumstances, his crew managed to construct two seaworthy vessels — only to have them claimed and reassigned elsewhere by the Spanish Crown. Cortez was not deterred: he rebuilt ships, and in the face of further erosions of progress due to disease and hostilities, persisted in exploring the coast.

Despite the vast scope of his efforts, the Spanish captain was not to be the first outsider to discover that Baja California was a peninsula rather than an island, nor did he ever reach Southern California. The first non-native to sail past Pt. Loma and into the splendid harbor at San Diego was a Portuguese-born mariner sailing under the Spanish flag — Juan Rodriguez Cabrillo.

Cabrillo's success was almost as unlikely as that of Cortez. He, too, overcame difficult obstacles including undersized ships, meager provisions, and an undisciplined crew. On the other hand, Cabrillo's advantage was his unparalleled skill as a sailor.

By carefully pacing his trip up the coast and putting in regularly to gather food, the Portuguese explorer not only sustained the expedition but reduced the incidence of scurvy that had been so costly to others. When he left San Diego, Cabrillo continued leisurely up the coast, landing at points now called San Pedro, Santa Monica, and Ventura. Such frequent stops also afforded him the opportunity to meet with local natives, to whom he presented gifts of friendship.

Cabrillo navigated even further up the coast, charting maps and keeping journals, and in general made a significant contribution to knowledge of the western seaboard. Among other places, he put in at Carpinteria and Point Conception, then headed northward. But, due to weather conditions, he missed Monterey and the San Francisco Bay. This is understandable to anyone who has knowledge of prevailing weather conditions there and knows how punishing this sea can be, quite in contrast to its name, "Pacific." Juan Cabrillo was not exempt. During bad weather the Portuguese explorer broke his arm in a fall, and although he continued the expedition, harsh weather, exposure, and poor medical attention overwhelmed him. On January 3, 1543, while in port on one of the Santa Barbara Channel Islands, Cabrillo died, his last energies spent urging his men to carry on his work. Under a new commander they did so, even if at greater expense to the natives, as the new commander did not share Cabrillo's appreciation of the people and the land.

While nautical traffic was being established along the coast, a parallel overland movement began proceeding north from Mexico City. These land and sea movements were given impetus by Royal Patronage — an agreement between the King of Spain and the Pope which gave to the King and to his military delegates in Mexico City the right to make final decisions on all matters (secular *and* sacred) within the colonial jurisdiction.

Three religious orders contributed to the northern overland advance: the Jesuits, the Dominicans, and the Franciscans — the Jesuits being politically and numerically the strongest. When the decision was made to establish a series of missions up the Baja coast in the hopes of discouraging other nations from taking too keen an interest in the lands, the Spanish officials approached the Jesuits. However, instead of simply issuing a command (which it was clearly their prerogative to do), they politely petitioned the Jesuits to undertake this task, offering to pay all the costs. At first the Order declined; later, they agreed on the condition that they build the missions at their *own* expense — *and* with the provision that they themselves were to be in charge of the soldiers and of all other matters secular and sacred. The government consented, and in 1697 a series of missions was begun on the peninsula of Baja California. This was by no means a small undertaking, as the work eventually spanned three quarters of a century. Progress came to an abrupt halt, however, when the Spanish government recalled all Jesuits under its domain in 1768. The reasons for this decision, while not necessarily applicable to the padres in Baja, were many and complex. At the heart of it, though, appears to have been a fear experienced throughout Europe that politically the Jesuits had become too powerful and had begun to pose a threat to the monarchy itself.

The order was therefore dismissed by the provincial

The Missions
of the
Baja
Peninsula

The Jesuits
Are
Expelled

governor, Captain Gaspar de Portola, and responsibility for northward expansion of the Baja project was offered to the Franciscans, under the charge of the newly appointed Superior, Father Junipero Serra.

The Sword
and
The Cross

Thus, the combination of the Sword and the Cross continued — this time, however, the Sword held sway as soldiers and missionaries traveled together into this new territory.

The purpose of these expeditions was clearly one of conquest. Whether they were willing or not, members of religious orders were assigned to all forward advances, and after a region was taken it became the responsibility of the missionaries to hold it. While the padres' salaries were paid by the officials in Mexico City, and although they were given assistance when first establishing a mission, it was understood that henceforth they were to look to themselves. They were assisted by a detachment of soldiers — sometimes half a dozen, sometimes more — but their major resources were their own wits and persuasive powers.

The Mission
Project

It was clear from the outset that though the padres and the soldiers worked toward a common goal their motivations and methods were quite different. The two groups were basically antithetical to each other: the padres proselytized; the soldiers let blood. As a group the priests were thought particularly "difficult" — one military governor observed that they demonstrated "less regimentation than might reasonably be expected from a box of puppies." On the Franciscans part, the missionaries could counter with the often-heard lament: "From soldiers, deliver us. O. Lord." Yet in order to achieve a measure of success, which at times meant simply surviving, both sides learned to be mutually tolerant. Progress continued to be made.

We have, then, the first implementation of a plan, originally in the hands of the Jesuits, calling for missions to be established from the tip of the Baja Peninsula and north to some point not yet specified. Eventually the missions would extend beyond the peninsula and into what was to become the state of California, making this a single venture involving what are now two divisions — Lower and Upper, Baja and Alta.

California
Is
Named

By nature this region is one land — an area of common typography and climate, bathed on its western side by the same waters. And, of course, both divisions do share the name of "California." It is not known how this name came about, and numerous authors have offered possible explanations. Some suggest that its origin is in the Latin word *califacio*, which means to heat or make warm, or the Catalan term *californo*, which may be translated as "hot oven." In Latin there is also *calidus* or *calida*, which one is tempted to associate with *fornax* — an oven, furnace, or kiln. The Spanish word *cal*, meaning "lime," might be juxtaposed with the Latin *fornax*, to suggest that California means "lime kiln."

But the most popular notion is that the word refers to a mythical island named California described in the old Spanish

19

novels *Amadis of Gaul* and *The Deeds of Esplandian*. In *Amadis* — a popular work of the 15th century — one learns of an island kingdom under the control of Califa, the Amazon queen, and her women subjects. After a series of swashbuckling adventures highlighted by combat with the Christian invaders, the queen loses her heart to the enemy Esplandian, son of the hero Amadis. The story is resolved when Califa and her Amazon companions become converts and present to the Christians their exotic island Calfornia.

———————————

The People:

The first Californians, which is to say those people indigenous to the land, had been making their homes there for some unknown number of centuries. While anthropologists continually push the date farther and farther into the past, there is no evidence to suggest that natives worry the matter — they know who they are, and in a substantive sense, from whence they came.

The sailors who went ashore from Cabrillo's ship found themselves among essentially gentle people. In this favored piece of geography, the way of life, too, was generally unstrained. Here, conscious of their good fortune and well-being, the California natives were in a state of grace; they were their own *Keepers of the Good Way.*

Although many small villages could be found at myriad points up and down the sunny coast, of particular favor were the numerous sheltered bays and those points where clear, shallow rivers emptied into the sea. Since natives were familiar with the healing qualities of the region's numerous hot springs, these too became popular home sites.

Housing styles varied with location, resulting in a wide range of construction techniques. Some tribes built earth-banked conical lodges with a center smoke hole, similar to the hide tipis associated with the people of the Plains, while others built elaborate thatched huts of bark, or redwood plank structures of a more permanent nature. But whatever style emerged, because of the temperate climate most activities were conducted out-of-doors.

Also because of this continuous warmth, clothing was practically unnecessary, although for comfort and convenience the women usually wore knee-length skirts, occasionally made of deerskin, but more often woven from the soft shredded bark of willow or cedar. Except for necklaces of bone, seashell, or small stones, nothing covered their breasts. Their hair was either parted in the middle, pulled to the back of the head and retained by a net, or braided and held with decorative ornaments. Paint was frequently applied to the face.

Both men and women wore sandals and, during cool weather, elegant robes of rabbit fur. Otherwise the men restricted their wardrobe to a small apron. Native children, too, dressed in accordance with the climate: in a manner fully appropriate to individuals who spent the eternal summer chasing butterflies, they wore only what nature had provided them at birth.

Native Dress

The people made each long day both productive and pleasurable. As part of their domestic chores, mothers frequently changed the soft grass or rabbit fur diapers of their children, who slept strapped to cradle boards.

Domestic Life

The women also manufactured baskets of all sizes and shapes. These served as common household containers as well as significant gift items, and some were so tightly woven that they were actually used for cooking vessels. Meat or fish was placed in baskets of water, hot rocks were then added, and the temperature quickly reached a boil.

A medley of food items was available to the indigenous Californians, one of the most important being an acorn-based bread which was always prepared in large quantities. Since edible nuts, roots, and berries were readily available, and since the men fished and hunted regularly, native economy was based on gathering rather than agriculture.

In terms of human values, these were a people to whom

existence was highly prized — *being* in itself was held to be most sacred. God — the great spirit — was to be found in and among the people and the things of nature, not out beyond the clouds. The two-legged beings, the four-legged beings, those that flew and those that swam all contained this spirit. God was indeed among them — the kingdom was at hand.

Native
Liturgy

The natives expressed these religious beliefs in rich ceremonials which reflected the cyclical quality of nature. Elaborate rituals signaled the evolution of life, the turn of the seasons, and the passage from child to adult. These were occasions to be celebrated by the entire village — they provided opportunities for feasting, singing, and dancing. The use of tobacco was also a part of native ceremonies. Straight tubular pipes, often carved of manzanita and lined with soapstone, were considered sacred vessels. A blend of tobaccos, each symbolizing an aspect of nature, was carefully arranged in the bowl. All the represented elements — the fish, the deer, the insects, the brown and green grass, etc. — were then pulled together by the fire of the Great Spirit. After the fusion, or communion, that occurred within both the pipe *and* its user, smoke was blown to the four sacred cardinal directions.

Young native men often sought a more private vision as part of their religious development. Sometimes aided by mescal or jimsonweed, but always aided by prayer, these

youths appropriated the qualities of the visionary image that appeared to them. Thus the future identity of the native youth was cast.

Other communal practices included rites of purification conducted in *sweat lodges.* Hemispherical frames held secure by long strands of tough grass were erected, and hide covers were added to create completely tight, dark, dome-shaped structures. Inside, water was poured over hot stones to generate the steam by which natives were physically and spiritually cleansed.

Many native customs involved intensive community interaction. For example, during the first years of marriage young couples alternated their residences, living first with one and then the other set of parents, exchanging gifts with their "hosts" each time they moved. This served as an interim period during which adjustments were made — the couple gained maturity while simultaneously collecting about them the household items necessary for a life together. Such ambilocal arrangements usually worked well, continuing until the couple gave birth to their first child, after which it was expected that the new family would move away to establish, finally, their own home.

Matters affecting the whole of the community were taken to Council gatherings, where decisions were made by majority vote. Here, people sought the wisdom of the aged and of those individuals possessing significant powers of observation or insight — usually medicine men. Balance of solemnity was maintained by hired clowns who routinely interrupted the meetings, mocking the speakers in such a way as to discourage self-righteousness and pomposity. Among the customs which defined social relationships, none was more ponderous than that of *naming*. Names were conferred upon individuals at various times during their lives, and with utmost care. As they represented the entree to the soul, these titles were not to be abused. Never was a name called out simply to gain a person's attention; rather, individuals were referred to tangentially, indirectly. After a native died, his name was never spoken again.

Native Regard for "Naming"

Furthermore, no familiar name was used to refer to "grandmother," who represented the source of all things potential. Nor was a personal name assigned to the "Great Spirit" — unlimited and boundless love. Yet during the mission period, those natives who learned the Sign of the Cross (or of the Father, Son, and Holy Spirit) recognized these as similar to well-established categories already at work in their own culture.

Customs and Traditions

Long before the coming of the Spaniards, natives had developed artistic techniques for dealing with the most profound of human experiences. Birth, growth, illness, and death were recapitulated in model by expert practitioners called "dry painters." Powerful iconoc images were created on beds of soft, clean sand as finely ground substances flowed between the thumb and first finger of the master. When completed, the images were integrated into a whole ritual which was generally, but not exclusively, conducted in

28

accordance with healing ceremonies. To drive sickness from the body, curing techniques required the patient to sit naked upon a particular image designed to absorb his or her specific illness. Although the skillfully rendered image was inevitably destroyed in the process, on no occasion were paintings expected to be preserved as "fine art." Instead, the practice itself was propagated through the apprentice system — technical information was passed on and skills were developed under the watchful eye of a master.

An equally important teaching "assignment" involved the communication of history, mythology, and survival to native youths. The responsibility of general education was thus entrusted to the elders. There were the techniques of hunting, fishing, medicine, and geography to be acquired, as well as a knowledge of the arts, laws, and traditions of the people. In lieu of written language, the primary device for carrying information forward was the tale, or story. Central to many of these was the outrageous character, *Coyote.* Coyote is a trickster figure — at times clever, at times the fool — to whom many of the present conditions of man are attributed. There was a period, for example, when all the stars in the sky were equally spaced in neat rows. It is the result of a foolish act by Coyote that they are now horribly disarranged! And once, because of an intense hunger, Coyote violated the wisdom of his elders by eating certain prohibited berries. The results were disasterous, and of considerable personal embarrassment! Other Coyote dilemmas included the taking of unwise counsel, and the reluctance to learn certain landmarks which would direct his path. He took shortcuts when preparing for the hunt, thereby ending up the hunted instead of the hunter.

Occasionally Coyote did manage to arrive at the proper solution to a problem, although native youngsters learned just as much (and howled with delight) when he blundered. By listening with rapt attention to each story recounted by village elders, children prepared themselves for responsible adulthood.

In all situations — scholastic, judicial, or spiritual — native Californians functioned with a powerful sense of community. Theirs was a *primary*, root, or radical culture. And as a result of their *prime* or primitive tradition, a communal wholeness existed. Within these small, closely knit societies each individual enjoyed an important membership; self-definition and self-importance were therefore achieved as a result of community relationships. In terms of cultural image, the native community was expressed as a living tree whose size and shape was constituted by the people standing together. Since the absence of even one person diminished this unity, the tree was careful to nourish and protect itself. And, because members functioned interdependently and the actions of a single individual could have profound impact on the whole, it was necessary to be individually responsible.

In relating to the tree each person saw himself or herself standing at a unique center — the heart of the individual was projected to that single point where the tree's vertical and horizontal axes intersect. No matter what size the community, each member enjoyed that same, yet singular position. California's natives knew *who* they were — and they knew *where* they were — because of this sacred tree at the center of the world.

————————————

THE TREE AT THE CENTER OF THE WORLD

The Cross was carried into California suspended from the belt of the fifty-five-year-old Father-President, Junipero Serra.

In 1769, one year after the Franciscans replaced the Jesuits, four expeditions left the Baja Peninsula for the Bay of San Diego, two groups traveling aboard the *San Carlos* and *San Antonio* and two detachments traveling by land. The group aboard the *San Antonio* was the first to reach its destination, while the other parties arrived at varying intervals. Padre Serra journeyed with one of these latter groups, accompanied by the provincial governor and military leader of the entire enterprise, Captain Gaspar de Portola. Traveling separately but under Father Serra's command was Father Juan Crespi, who arrived about two weeks before the Father-President. This *very remarkable priest was Father Serra's student and later his colleague, intimate, and confessor. His contribution to the missions was to prove considerable. Nonetheless, the final responsibility for all sacred matters was held by Junipero Serra. He was the force, the man of imagination, the person called forward to provide wisdom and counsel during this formidable undertaking.*

The trip from Baja, today considered a comfortable weekend respite, cost dearly in 1769. The *San Antonio* required fifty-five days to reach its destination and the *San Carlos* took one hundred and ten. Everyone on board had scurvy; twenty-four had died at sea. Of those who stepped ashore in San Diego all were "skin and bones" and most had lost their teeth; the expedition, though composed of men under thirty, appeared aged and infirm. A water shortage and the loss of several horses and mules caused similar problems for the land parties.

About 120 men, only half of those who had left Baja, made it to San Diego. Once on the beach, this sickly group unloaded the numerous seeds of their future settlement: church paraphernalia, books, tools, trade items, food, and dry goods. At night the crew tended sick and injured livestock.

As the priests themselves had all managed to arrive in decent health, there was naturally a great thanksgiving on the day Junipero Serra arrived safely in San Diego — July 1, 1769. Together again were Fathers Juan Viscaino, Fernando Parron, Francis Gomez, Juan Crespi, and the Father-President.

On Sunday, the next day, Father Serra celebrated a solemn High Mass in honor of the reunion.

In addition to soldiers and clergy, the expedition included blacksmiths, bakers, cooks, muleteers, carpenters, and a physician — Pedro Pratt — whose chief responsibility was to shave the officers each morning. Although he was sometimes called upon to remove bullets and arrows as well, Dr. Pratt's medical skills were limited to the simplest of treatments, and in his surgical methods he employed the most rudimentary of techniques. Father Serra himself, suffering from a large ulcer on his leg, had to turn to a muleteer, who relieved his pain with medications and techniques developed for treating animals.

In reality the padre arrived to find himself in charge of an infirmary. In general, the art of medicine as practiced by the Spaniards was crude and not at all respected. Serious illnesses therefore eventually had to be referred to native doctors who had developed more sophisticated cures. The expedition was further forced to rely heavily on the good will of local people when their supplies dwindled, and they traded clothing and simple jewelry to obtain fish and deer meat. Of course, there were factions among the natives: many were curious yet generous, making the newcomers welcome, while others remained deeply offended by the intrusion. To inhibit the community which threatened to develop within their midst, this latter group quickly organized a series of raids that proved considerably frustrating for priests and soldiers

37

alike. Under cover of night, several natives once rowed into the bay and cut the ropes which held the ships at anchor. Some boldly pirated away dry goods; others stole the very sheets from beneath bed-ridden soldiers helpless with scurvy. And during the day, hostile natives routinely fired arrows in the direction of settlers who happened to have gathered for conversation.

This harassment could have been more severe, and probably would have been, if it were not for the strange disease that so debilitated the Spaniards. Under the threat of scurvy the natives were a little nervous; they feared that they too might contract the sickness, and most thought it wise to maintain some distance.

Throughout this cautious though genuine harassment, the dedicated Fr. Crespi moved openly among the natives in order to establish good relations and gain a command of the language. When able to engage in conversation, the padre began collecting lists of words he believed to be nouns, while simultaneously presenting gifts to his new acquaintances. Realizing that the young learn languages with ease, he then worked vigorously to gain the friendship of a young boy in the hope of teaching him Spanish. This project was successful: during the years that followed the young man became a trusted friend and the official interpreter for the missionaries.

At the same time that these events were unfolding in California's wilderness, the American Colonies were only seven years from gaining independence from Great Britain. Numerous cities in the east already displayed advanced architecture, and a lively trade of goods from throughout the known world was being maintained. The streets were filled with fine horses and handsome carriages; there even existed a cultural hour during which English tea was drunk by distinguished company in fine dress.

By contrast, in California daily life often involved fierce struggles just to stay alive, and the famous grey robes worn by Father Serra and the other Franciscans had now become worn and patched.

This famous missionary had originally come from the island of Mallorca located off the coast of Spain. He was born and raised in Petra, a village whose numerous bleached sandstone houses appear so determinedly unsympathetic to children. The padre's own home, No. 6 Calle Barraca Alta, is now a memorial and may be visited by the public.

Fr. Junipero Serra, O.F.M.

It was this small, deeply Catholic community that Miguel Jose Serra left to enter the Order of Franciscans. In 1730, at the age of seventeen, he chose the name Junipero ("Juniper") in honor of the trees which filled the forests of his native Mallorca — trees that had served him as a source of inspiration.

As his preaching talents became apparent, Fr. Serra was given the opportunity to complete his education at Palma, eventually earning a Doctor of Theology degree from Lullian

University there. Though considered rather shy and reserved in manner, his energy and devotion to work generated a fierce loyalty shared by all who served at his side throughout the years.

Upon receiving permission to enter missionary service in 1749 Fr. Serra was assigned to Mexico. For nearly a decade he worked in the rugged and inhospitable regions of Queretaro. During the next ten years he worked at a variety of assignments, the culmination of which was his appointment as Superior and President.

Doctor and professor *de prima* of sacred theology, commissary of the holy office, and president of all missions: this was the Reverend Father Fray Junipero Serra, the man who on July 16, 1769, with the aid of Padres Vizcaino and Parron, slowly ascended the hill overlooking San Diego harbor and fashioned a large wooden cross to mark the site of the first mission in California. Working together on the hill, the three men dug a hole eight and one-half feet into the earth. Here, they planted the soaring cross — the sacred tree at the center of the world.

———————

A Tree Takes Root:
Mission San Diego de Alcala

We can't know if Fr. Junipero Serra ever consciously said this, but his personal maxim well could have been, "I'll see it when I believe it." For, whenever the padre determined that something was needed — be it the solution to an architectural problem or a way to gather food — it seemed to heave into sight. While some might not recommend this approach as a

Opposite page:
The Holy Infant
of Atocha

43

viable technique for "getting on" in the world, it worked infinitely well for the famous padre, perhaps because he, like the natives he had come to serve, also saw the presence of God in the individuals and objects around him, and knew that the kingdom was, truly, at hand.

This attitude is reflected in the physical structures at the missions, where *bricolage* or improvisation often had to take precedence over engineering, and where Native Americans displayed considerable creativity in solving architectural problems, particularly since the proper tools and materials were often not available.

Mission
Structures

Still, in San Diego, Fr. Serra's first efforts were quite modest: a series of crude huts was hastily erected, one of which served as the first church. A bell was suspended from the limb of a tree.

The later, more permanent mission buildings were constructed of adobe. Under the padres' supervision, natives filled numerous wooden molds with a wet and sticky combination of clay, manure, and straw. Heat from the sun then transformed the mixture into firm, rectangular bricks with which sturdy dwellings could be built. However, as the missionaries were yet unaware of California's powerful and destructive earthquakes, the walls of these first structures were not sufficiently thick.

After the principal partitions of a mission building went up, beams were added and the roof was thatched with dry straw or tule. The interior was painted, maguey mats were hung in doorways, and the building was then considered complete. This was the authentic mission architecture; the tile roofs that have come to be characteristic of most structures were added only later — as recollections of Spain, perhaps, but most definitely as protection against attack. For hostile natives had quickly discovered that an entire mission complex could be destroyed by a few flaming arrows directed to the dry tule roofs. Something more substantial than straw was obviously in order. Since such aggressions were a fact of life, and food supplies often dwindled dangerously, success for the hillside mission near San Diego Bay was not immediate, and certainly not assured.

Soon after his arrival at San Diego Bay, Captain Gaspar de Portola, the governor and military leader of the California expedition, began the second phase of the mission plan. Leaving Fr. Serra in San Diego, Portola headed overland on July 14, 1769, hoping to establish a facility at Monterey Bay.

Six months passed before Portola appeared again in San Diego, his efforts toward Monterey having proved unsuccessful. Annoyed and frustrated upon returning, he found conditions in Fr. Serra's San Diego Mission "hopeless." Matters were in fact quite desperate — deaths and disease continued to occur, and the natives were not at all eager to embrace Christianity. Portola gave orders to abandon the whole project should supplies and reinforcements not arrive before March 19, the feast day of St. Joseph. To the missionaries' good fortune, however, a ship did arrive in time, and at least in terms of subsistence things were never again quite so bleak.

Subsequently, cattle were brought overland from Mexico and additional priests arrived to assist with the mission task. Gardens were planted, canals built, and a substantial palisade was constructed to protect the mission compound.

Intermittent acts of aggression nonetheless continued. In fact, a significant confrontation had occurred while Captain Portola was yet absent from San Diego. The routine of the community was shattered when from the surrounding hills a group of angry natives descended upon the mission and attempted to rid the area of the intruders. Only a few military guards were present when the natives attacked with their simple weapons, but they quickly answered with guns. The "Leather Jackets" with their muskets easily routed the natives, and the battle ended in minutes. But its effect was longterm. From this time forward firearms were to play an essential role in "Indian diplomacy." The date was August 15, 1769 — the date of the Assumption of the Blessed Virgin.

Despite such melees, the majority of natives at San Diego Bay were cooperative; many displayed an eagerness to assist with various construction tasks and to share regular meals with the padres. Community development remained slow, however, and a full year passed before the first baptism. Father Serra did come close on one previous occasion, but just as the holy water was about to flow, the parents wrenched the child from the padre's hands. Father Serra

blamed himself and, in the years that followed reflected with pain upon the incident.

I charge you,
daughters of Jerusalem,
by the gazelles, by the hinds of the field,
not to stir my love, nor rouse it,
until it please to awake.
—The Song of Songs

While local relationships between the natives and padres were sometimes strained, this was nothing compared to tension between the natives and the soldiers. Due to a mutual lack of respect, life was shot through with fear, hatred, and suspicion. Community development was impossible under these circumstances, and the padres determined that it was necessary to separate the natives — and themselves — from the military. Thus, about six miles up the valley a new site was identified: the soil was good — it was, in fact, a better location. Soldiers remaining on the original hill continued construction of what finally became a substantial fort — the "presidio" — and with the exception of a few storerooms retained by the padres, the entire compound fell exclusively to military use. Meanwhile, in the company of a group of friendly natives, many of whom were now converts to Christianity, the missionaries established themselves at the new site.

The Mission
Is
Relocated

47

Relocation proved effective. A sense of trust soon developed as sympathetic natives began to spend their days and then their nights within the compound. To unite the new community its members quickly built a church of tall posts topped by a tule roof; natives and missionaries now had a place in which to celebrate their lives together. Following a plan outlined by Fr. Serra, the new Christians also constructed homes for themselves, a residence for the padres, and quarters for the civilian muleteers and shepherds who had come to join them. They built a granary and a shop for the smith. Local women were instructed in the art of spinning and weaving by families of native converts who were brought up from Mexico.

The indigenous Californians learned new things quickly from the missionaries, and they were fascinated by aspects of Spanish culture which seemed to parallel their own beliefs and concerns. They revered fecundity; and once, at San Diego de Alcala, a group of women whose homes were well removed from the mission presented a request to see the sacred Mother and Child. It was clear the women had learned that the mission maintained an image of Mary and Jesus. The padres were pleased to show it, but being not at all certain of the intentions of the natives, they took precautions to protect the image. The picture of Mary and the Child was brought outside and displayed from behind a post fence. Actually, the women had no thought of harming the picture; they were in fact delighted to see it. Unable to communicate in Spanish, they nonetheless demonstrated that they understood and respected the idea of the eternal mother and child by pressing their bare breasts between the posts toward the picture.

Religious images were an important part of the message that the Franciscans brought into California. Indeed, items ranging from simple souvenirs to objects of great complexity and dimensionality were carried in by the crate-load. Characteristic of all these, however, was the implication of values that transcended the quality of the individual object itself. The pieces — saints, crosses, fonts, paintings, and pictures — were all, as it were, transparent: they embodied ideas, and like the priests themselves, represented European culture, universal Catholicism, and the church hierarchy. In coming to California these objects brought the Church to the church.

In 1774, Mission San Diego de Alcala reached its fifth year, but conditions were never totally secure. Each day did bring greater strength to the community, and new converts were made in large numbers (sometimes fifty at a time). Still, some groups of the native population were clearly antagonistic, and while others appeared genuinely indifferent, it was difficult to gauge the feelings and loyalties of the remaining natives — the majority — a disconcerting situation.

Meanwhile, the hostile natives, aware that the community was gaining in strength, determined that the hour had come to rid themselves of these intruders lest the missionaries become permanent guests. They sent runners to other native villages and secretly enlisted armed support. At one o'clock on the morning of November 5, 1775, the conspiracy came off — a raiding party of perhaps a thousand men crept over the rise behind the mission and fell upon the sleeping compound. One group set fire to the outside of the buildings while others busied themselves looting trunks and wardrobes. The fire awakened Fr. Vincente Fuster and Fr. Luis Jayme. Still clutching his robe with one hand, Fr. Jayme burst out of his quarters startling natives with shouts of "Amar a Dios, Hijos!" — "Love God, my children!" Attackers immediately dragged him through wet leaves to the bottom of a hill in front of the mission, where they beat his naked body with clubs and shot him with with no less than eighteen arrows. When the padre was found the next morning, only his hands remained unabused; in an act of piety these were separated from his body and preserved at the mission.

Among others who received mortal wounds on this day was a carpenter named Ursulino. When pierced by an arrow, Ursulino realized his life had come to an end, and called out to the natives exclaiming, "Ha, Indian, you have killed me. God forgive you!" During the five days that he remained alive the carpenter prepared a will in which he requested that his worldly goods be used for the natives and the development of Mission San Diego de Alcala.

Thus, his attitude reflected the strength of the values which Father Serra promoted and instilled in his followers, a tenacity which allowed this and other missions to endure.

Personages at the Tree:

Mission San Carlos Borromeo de Carmelo (Monterey)

Military Governor Portola had failed in his first attempt to establish a mission at Monterey, but he did not let a year pass before organizing a second effort. Thus, in mid-April of 1770, two groups departed from San Diego, Fr. Serra traveling aboard the packet *San Antonio*, and Captain Portola leading the overland excursion. It took almost forty days for the land

53

party to reach that point near the edge of the bay where Portola's earlier expedition had turned back.

As they approached this site, soldiers set out to find the marker that had been planted on the previous visit. After several minutes of wandering through tall grasses, one of the men called out. The party fell silent as it approached, for in the center of a small clearing not far from the inreaches of the sea stood the four foot cross, around which lay a circular carpet of arrows, all of them pointing to the cross at the center. The entire spot had obviously been embellished by local natives. Clusters of eagle feathers had been pressed into the soil at seemingly random intervals. And hanging from the cross was a string of fresh, silver sardines, under which lay a small, neatly arranged mound of mussels. It was clear that the image of the cross was potent to the natives. Fully expecting the cross to have been destroyed, the soldiers could only wonder about the unusual respect that was in evidence.

The party then traveled on through groves of pine and cypress, eventually settling on the beach not far from where the Carmelo River empties into the sea. There they awaited the arrival of Fr. Serra and the ship *San Antonio*. When the tiny black shape appeared a week later, Portola ordered three large signal fires to be built on the beach, according to a previously arranged communication plan. At length, a salvo from the ship's cannon acknowledged that the two parties were finally together at their destination.

Fr. Serra and Captain Portola proved equally enthusiastic

about the location, and decided to establish a large presidio there. In the name of the King, Portola took official possession of the port at Monterey, and all hands set to work on the new facility. Buildings went up and a palisade was constructed. Fr. Serra functioned out of a single room which served as his office, his quarters, and as the community church.

The natives of Monterey Bay were generally hospitable and worked cooperatively with the padres. But success would not be achieved easily. A situation developed here similar to that in San Diego — the Monterey natives, too, distrusted Leather Jacket soldiers. Fr. Serra elected to separate the mission functions from those of the armed garrison, and in 1771, a year after the founding of the original Monterey facility, the padres chose a new site about five miles away. Since it offered fresh water, more fertile soil, and a closer proximity to the sea, Carmelo was a better site.

Junipero Serra himself carried the statue of La Purisima — the Holy Virgin — to Carmel. Though in fact a man of small stature, standing no more than 5 feet 2 inches in height, he seemed of immense proportion indeed as he led the procession away from the presidio and toward the new location. Meanwhile, a new secular community developed around the presidio.

Since the weather on this favored peninsula agreed with his own physical well-being, Fr. Serra soon declared the new mission to be headquarters for the entire chain. Truly, he

21 SAN FRANCISCO DE SOLANO
20 SAN RAFAEL ARCANGEL
6 SAN FRANCISCO DE ASIS
14 SAN JOSE
8 SANTA CLARA
12 SANTA CRUZ
15 SAN JUAN BAUTISTA
2 SAN CARLOS BORROMEO DE CARMELO
3 SAN ANTONIO DE PADUA
16 SAN MIGUEL ARCANGEL
5 SAN LUIS OBISPO DE TOLOSA
11 LA PURISIMA CONCEPCION
19 SANTA INES
10 SANTA BARBARA
9 SAN BUENAVENTURA
17 SAN FERNANDO REY DE ESPANA
4 SAN GABRIEL ARCANGEL
7 SAN JUAN CAPISTRANO
18a SAN ANTONIO DE PALA
18 SAN LUIS REY DE FRANCIA
1 SAN DIEGO DE ALCALA

loved Carmel. Though his duties as Father-President continually demanded his presence at other facilities, the padre always returned to the warmth and simplicity of his small quarters at Carmel, quarters which he furnished simply: a table with candlestick, a chair, a wooden cot, a gourd, and his favorite rosary.

The New
Community

The community at Carmel grew rapidly — throughout the years seven churches were constructed in all. Though Fr. Serra contributed ideas and suggestions for what has become the basilica, he did not live to see realized the present structure, the "new church." This project was begun in 1793 under the architectural supervision of Manuel Ruez, a highly respected master mason. Hundreds of native converts who comprised the membership of San Carlos Borromeo de Carmelo undertook the construction; thus, it was really the native hand that formed the character of the place. The window above the main door attracts particular attention, due to its powerful symbolic function. Rectangular in design and placed at an angle, the glass appears to be warped — being neither square, level, flat, true, nor plumb. Over the years visitors have described the window as representing a star, a rose, a butterfly, the cardinal directions, or the cross. Some authors argue that it is a native image, commonly found on shield covers.

By the early 1800's Carmel, like other California missions, had amassed a sufficient amount of material goods to attract the attention of the disreputable pirate, Hyppolite de Bouchard.

Bouchard was a genuine sea marauder. Though his written ultimatums for food, wine, and other stores indicate a certain charm and grace, he was nonetheless a man to be taken seriously. Daring daylight raids on coastal communities reinforced his reputation for unprincipled boldness.

Hyppolite de Bouchard

In November of 1818 Bouchard's two ships were sighted off the coast of Monterey, thus creating a general panic during which the community of San Carlos Borromeo de Carmelo abandoned their mission and moved inland for safety. When the pirate landed, his men ransacked Monterey's presidio and new secular community, but for reasons not at all apparent, spared the Carmelo mission.

Since the founding of Monterey marked the end of Captain Gaspar de Portola's contribution to the missions, it would be appropriate to pause and consider the man and his career. After the establishment of the second mission, Portola was appointed mayor of the Mexican city of Puebla, where he served for seven years before returning to Spain and a life of retirement and obscurity.

Captain Gaspar de Portola

A native of Balageur, Spain, Portola entered a regiment of dragoons in 1734, at the age of eleven. Before his assignment to Mexico, he served Spain in raids upon Portugal and distinguished himself in a campaign against Italy. He was forty-four when General Galvez appointed him Governor of the Californias.

This dark, hawkish man proved a capable administrator whose sensitivity to the needs of those in his charge allowed him to accomplish much through good will. He believed that in the great span of history the mission effort was significant, that the courage and dedication of priests and soldiers together would make a difference.

A nobleman with a keen sense of tradition, he was alert to occasions of ceremony. Among his final official acts, Portola unfurled on the beach at Monterey the standard of His Catholic Majesty, Don Carlos III, and with polished and glistening sword ceremoniously extracted herbs from the earth. He then threw stones to the four cardinal directions, and in the royal name of Spain laid claim to the ground on which he stood.

———————————

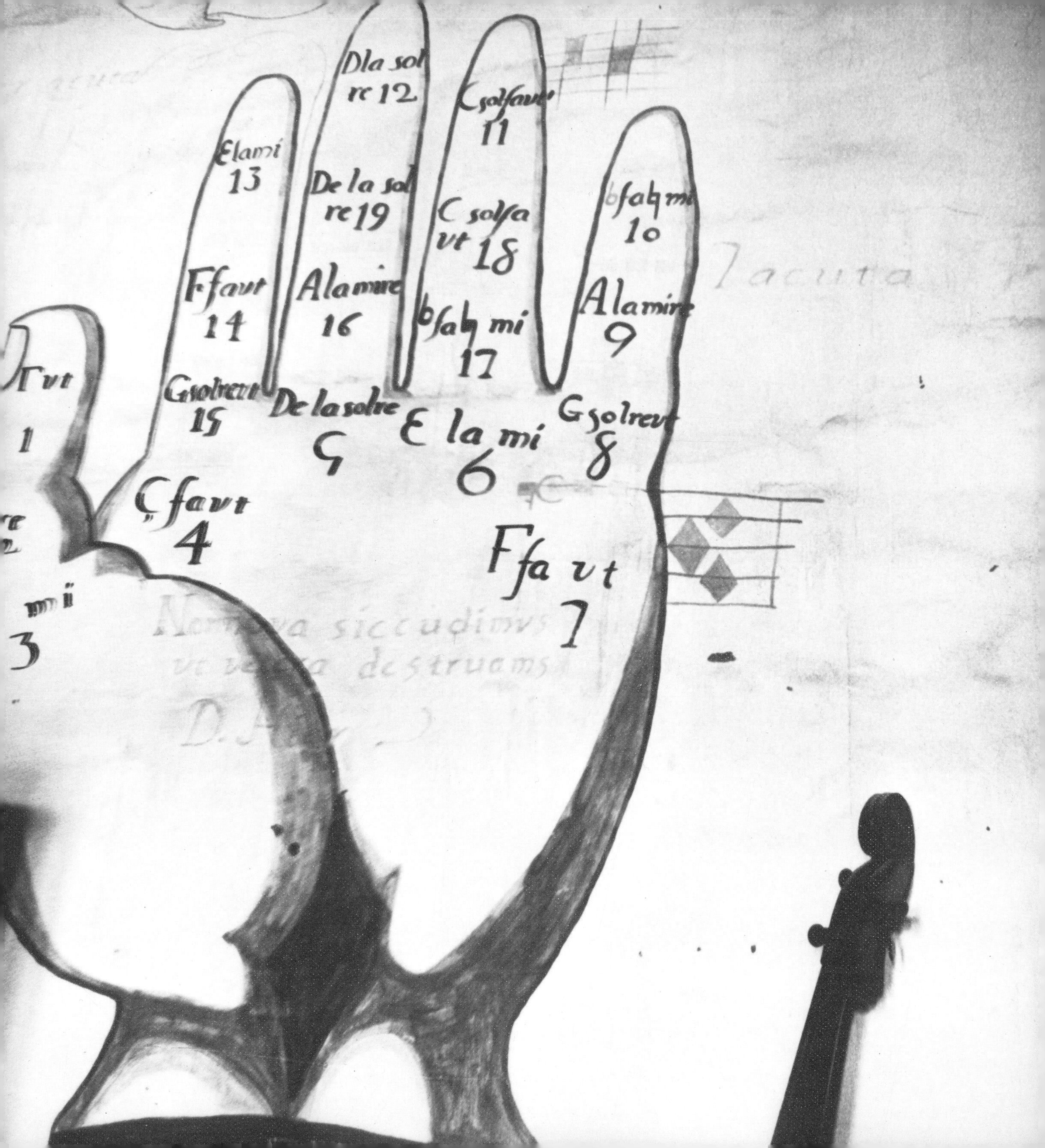
Γ ut
1
Dla sol re 12
Elami
13
De la sol re 19
C solfaut
11
C solfa ut 18
bfa♮mi
10
Ffaut
14
Alamire
16
bfa♮ mi
17
Alamire
9
Gsolreut
15
De la solre
5
E la mi
6
G solreut
8
Cfaut
4
Ffa ut
7
mi
3

The Trade-Off Begins:
Mission San Antonio de Padua

Before completing his work at Carmelo, the Father-President became anxious to further mission development. Thus, in July of 1771, he led an expedition into the Santa Lucia mountains where a suitable glen was discovered. Though quite warm in midsummer, this was a pleasant place — the surrounding region, served by the Salinas River, contained a wide variety of trees including lupine, alders, willows, and particularly

*Opposite page:
Device for
Music
Instruction*

61

oaks. Fr. Serra thus named the area Los Robles — "The Oaks."

A number of native converts, a detachment of soldiers, and Padres Miguel Pieras and Buenaventura Sitjar were with him on this venture. However, Fr. Serra's stay was brief; soon after the founding ceremony he moved on, leaving Padre Pieras and Padre Sitjar to man the mission. As had been previously determined, the new outpost honored the name of Anthony of Padua, the popular thirteenth century Franciscan noted for his theological and rhetorical achievements as well as his connection with supernatural events. In one of the many stories concerning St. Anthony, we discover that in his company a small mule once knelt and prayed before the Blessed Sacrament! In another we are told that Anthony was seen holding the Christ child in his arms.

St. Anthony of Padua

It is therefore appropriate that one of the most bizarre incidents in mission history occurred at Mission San Antonio de Padua. The story tells of a native woman named Agueda — reputed to be over one hundred years of age — who presented herself to the mission priests with a request that she be baptized and accepted into the faith. When pressed for an explanation, Agueda revealed that other religious men had come years before wearing similar costumes and bringing the Christian message. These had urged her baptism. When asked in what manner these early priests had arrived, she reported that they had come from the sky — in what today would be described as a spaceship!

The founding of this mission also began in an unusual way. On the day of the founding of Mission San Antonio de Padua — July 14, 1771 — Fr. Serra's colleagues became concerned for his senses, as it was with apparently unfounded optimism that he rang a bell which hung from the limb of an oak. The other priests thought it queer that the Father-President should issue a call to people who were not there, to come to a church that was not there. But there were people nearby, and they did hear the bell, and they did come.

Within two weeks natives began building and forming the community of Mission San Antonio de Padua. As buildings went up and the palisade was erected, a lifestyle developed — a pattern of sharing that was to obtain at the other missions as well.

The New Community

Those natives who were attracted to the padres and to mission life settled in or around the facility. Other natives remained distrustful, but being more prudent than hostile, simply removed themselves to the hills and beyond. The families that did join the community frequently made their homes just outside the mission complex by constructing, as they had in the past, conical huts not unlike the plains tipis. These were indeed architectural marvels. During warm periods one foot of the outer covering was removed all the way around the bottom edge of the dwelling. The center smoke hole made the entire dwelling something of a giant flue, so that air in motion entered next to the earth, circulated within the lodge, then rose up and out the smoke hole. In this way

64

the natives enjoyed whatever breeze that was on the land, as if they made their homes around a small fire in a superbly designed fireplace.

The padres were originally unfamiliar with this principle and enjoyed relief only when cool air arrived in the evening. They slept quite soundly then, exhausted by the work and heat of the day.

Although a good deal of time passed before the priests completely understood their new home, what had first seemed like a wasteland slowly began to unfold as a splendid garden. Still, at the end of each day, the missionaries were careful to measure and distribute small portions of flour. Each person in the community made his own tortillas, while with an eye to the larder, dry biscuits and bits of chocolate were passed among them. Constantly benefiting from native instruction, the padres and soldiers appreciated an almost endless supply of nuts, seeds, herbs, and berries identified and contributed by local people.

Mission life naturally involved cultural exchanges. Lifestyles merged or conformed to each other; both native and European traditions were shared by community members. One eventual consequence of this adjustment concerned the names by which native converts came to be known. Throughout almost all of indigenous America, natives originally knew themselves as "The People." When the name of a tribe is translated, this is most frequently the meaning. Those who joined mission communities, however, relinquished their former titles and accepted instead the name of the mission with which they were associated. Hence, the natives in San Diego became known as *Diegueno*, and those at San Luis Rey became *Luiseno*. This gave rise to the term "Mission Indians."

The Significance
of
"Naming"

Personal names were also assigned to each native at the time of baptism. These were not grounded in nature as was the custom in most tribes; rather, the new names were selected from the Spanish tradition that had intervened, examples being, of course, *Jose, Miguel*, etc. Since the list of possibilities was not long, a second name was imposed in order to distinguish one "Jose" from another. This last name most often reflected the occupation or trade that a native engaged in, examples of ordinary mission names being *Joe Baker, James Carpenter*, and *Michael Smith*.

All elements of language were, in fact, immediate, pressing concerns in mission life. At San Antonio de Padua, for instance, Fr. Sitjar assembled a dictionary of native words and within a month of his arrival was preaching in the native tongue. (Each padre assigned to the California missions was actually expected to have gained a command of the native language within one year of his appointment.) But the language that finally came to be spoken throughout all the missions was, however, a polyglot — a kind of strange dialect containing words drawn from both Spanish and the variety of regional languages. This happened more by accident than design, but as the dialect was reasonably easy to learn it became common to all the mission communities.

A New
Language

While there were many such important similarities among the California missions, each was also distinctive. San Antonio de Padua, for example, became noted for its wealth and music, and particularly for the splendid horses it bred and maintained. At one time the mission owned over 350 of these prized animals. Endowed with beauty, strength, and courage, they soon became a temptation beyond endurance and though mission life was conducted with constant attention to the corrals, the horses disappeared with painful regularity.

Nonetheless, Mission San Antonio de Padua flourished. Before 1830, more than 4,500 baptisms were recorded and the padres had performed 1,100 weddings. The mission's cattle holdings were extensive, and the community owned 10,000 sheep.

A sharing of traditions grew more and more evident. Natives provided the new settlers with food and medications, folklore and cosmologies, while the Spaniards contributed information on agriculture and husbandry, as well as instruction in various trades and crafts previously unknown to the local people. Roman Catholicism, the faith which bound the community, found new expression in native terms — the liturgy was celebrated in the native tongue, and the Holy Virgin was painted with a native face.

The Horses of Mission San Antonio de Padua

67

A Tree at the Crossroads:
Mission San Gabriel Arcangel

Of the twenty-one Franciscan Missions, three honor the names of the Archangels: St. Gabriel, St. Michael, and St. Raphael. As entities, angels exist in nine ascending choirs: Angels, Archangels, Principalities, Powers, Virtues, Dominations, Thrones, Cherubim, and Seraphim. Raphael is understood to mean "God has healed," while Michael is

69

thought a question: "Who is like to God?" Gabriel, the angel who carried the message to Mary that she would become the mother of the Son of the Most High, means "man of God." How very sad that Mission San Gabriel was the site of one of the most deplorable incidents in all of mission history. Without negating the many positive exchanges that occurred between Native America and the Spaniards, it is a fact that some inevitably ended in tragedy.

The site for Mission San Gabriel Arcangel was chosen by Father Serra in 1771 at a place close to a large population of natives living near the Rio de los Temblores (so named because of the frequency of earthquakes). The location also enjoyed a strategic position at the intersection of the road from Mexico and the California north-south trail. The responsibility for founding a mission there was given to Fathers Angel Somera and Pedro Cambon.

By this time, a pattern had emerged for the founding of a mission. Two priests — one a senior member with previous mission experience and one a younger, less seasoned padre — accompanied the Father-President and a detachment of soldiers to the future mission site. After the founding ceremony, conducted by the Father-President, the senior priest took charge of the facility.

In this case, however, the standard procedure was not followed. Father Serra was occupied elsewhere at that time, and the full responsibility for the proceedings fell upon Frs. Somera and Cambon. They set forth from San Diego on

August 6, 1771, accompanied by fourteen soldiers and four muleteers. Following behind slow-moving cattle which they were bringing to the new site, the party took a month to reach their destination. At this time Fr. Somera identified a well-wooded spot served by at least an occasional creek.

As the padres hung their bell from the limb of a tree, several natives gathered to watch the proceedings. A decorated banner displaying an image of La Purisima — the Holy Virgin — drew particular attention. The natives considered it intently and showed genuine respect for those who carried it. Still, many of the local residents remained distant, satisfying their curiosities from more remote positions half hidden by the trees. At length, one of the soldiers was able to persuade a certain young woman of considerable charm and beauty to give up her place of hiding and come forward. No sooner did she comply than the soldier began to entertain himself — and the others — at the woman's expense by addressing her with vulgar and suggestive remarks. Unable to understand his language, she simply smiled. The soldier then began to rub her breasts and make advances beneath her skirt while the young woman stood frozen in terror. Although the padres did not witness this event, the natives did. They quickly came forward, gathered her up, and left the area. The soldiers roared with delight.

Little time passed before the soldiers discovered that the woman's husband, a local tribal leader, planned to hold the offender accountable for his outrageous actions. Thus, at the first opportunity a handful of natives confronted the entire detachment, and, in the melee that followed, the insulted husband was killed. Deciding that the best way to avoid future aggressions was to use this incident as an object lesson, the soldiers cut off the tribal leader's head and mounted it on top of a high pole for all to see. The natives returned at length, but only to petition for their property. With their leader properly buried, they withdrew, determined to have no future associations with the Spaniards.

Because of this incident, progress as measured by baptisms was very slow at San Gabriel, and the padres were years in winning the confidence of the natives. In time, however, a sense of trust was established and converts were made. Native members of the community of San Gabriel eventually constructed a church fifty-four feet long and eighteen feet wide, as well as a wooden house for the missionaries, a storeroom for general use, a kitchen, and fourteen other buildings surrounded by an adobe palisade. Still, the ugly

confrontation was not to be forgotten; this was an unhappy place. Therefore, in 1776 (the year that the American colonies declared their independence) the community of San Gabriel moved out to relocate on the present site — a few miles from the original mission. Here, life was indeed more properous. By 1800, almost 2,000 natives had been baptized and over 1,000 were making their homes at the mission. Also in 1800, the chapel that presently stands there was built.

To manage their affairs, the relocated community pressed

into service Mrs. Eubalia Perez — the wife of a soldier — as controller of all secular matters, including the maintenance of mission funds and the overseeing of mission activities. Mrs. Perez was an organizational wizard, and under her leadership San Gabriel became an agricultural and industrial model. The community constructed a grist mill and a carpenter's shop; they built a facility for making soap and candles, and another for leatherwork and weaving. The padres even arranged to have an artist brought from Mexico to provide instruction in drawing and painting. The mission maintained over 40,000 animals — mostly cattle — as well as hundreds of acres of garden around which a twelve-foot-high, fruit-bearing cactus fence had been planted. Both wine and brandy were produced on the grounds.

San Gabriel soon became noted for its gracious hospitality. The success and prosperity achieved at this mission was shared with all travelers who stopped to rest at the junction of the north-south and east-west highways. It was soon necessary to construct more extensive accommodations to provide for both the famous and infamous guests of the community — those who paused briefly, and those who stayed on, at Mission San Gabriel.

———————

"Coyote was walking down the road one day and it occurred to him that there was no one around but himself. So he went to his house under a tree, determined to make some other people. He first built a large oven; he made it of clay and it was round like the top half of an egg because good things come from eggs. He then made bread batter, and from it he fashioned a great number of small people. Coyote made a bed of charcoals in the oven and he looked at all the people he had made. 'I have made so many that I shall have to bake three times,' he said. He placed some of the people on a board, put them in the oven, and sealed the door. 'Now I shall just have to wait.' Coyote decided to rest his eyes for awhile, without falling asleep. But he did fall asleep. When he woke up he quickly pulled away the door and removed the board. The people were burned black. But they jumped up and ran away. Coyote knew that on earth there were black people.

"Then he put some more people on the board, put them in the oven, and sealed the door. 'I shall be careful not to cook them too much,' he said. And he got so nervous that he opened the door too soon. He pulled out the board and the people were still white, looking very pale. But the people jumped up and ran away. Coyote knew that on earth there were white people.

"Coyote was very disappointed but he tried once more. He put some people on the board, put them in the oven, and sealed the door. Coyote sang his sacred song and when the song was done he opened the door. He removed the board and the people were reddish brown — the color of perfect bread! These people became his friends and they made their homes for many years at that place where Mission San Gabriel was built. And that is the end of this story."

External Influences:

Mission San Luis Obispo de Tolosa

Father Junipero Serra, the little giant from Mallorca, held at
his disposal air, earth, fire, and water. The padre also
possessed a mythic history — a sense of the present and a
sense of the yon. We must allow that he enjoyed considerable
grace.

Opposite page:
Native Tile

77

In 1771, almost immediately after the founding of Carmel, the Father-President requested that a "wide and generous trail" be identified and maintained as the overland supply route from San Diego to Monterey. This "Royal Road," *El Camino Real* or the "King's Highway" as it came to be called, would eventually link the missions from San Diego to Sonoma. Civil communities (pueblos) and four major forts (presidios) would be situated along its route.

Once identified, the Royal Road was routinely maintained by the natives who comprised mission communities. These laborers spent their days clearing the trail of the overgrowth that had not been brought down by the movement of livestock. After each day's work they returned to their mission homes.

El Camino Real

Fr. Serra's notion of a highway had actually been inspired by the "caminos reales" of Spain — grand roadways constructed by order of King Ferdinand. California's Royal Road, however, was more like a wide path than a proper highway. And while the original highways had been assigned special police to protect travelers, "El Camino Real" enjoyed no such security. Each bend in the road was necessarily approached with suspicion, and each large boulder was regarded as the potential hiding place for a clutch of bandits.

The new road passed through a valley known to the natives as Tixlina, but which soldiers had named *Canada de los Osos* — "The Valley of the Bears." Here, in honor of Saint Louis, Bishop of Toulouse, Fr. Serra founded the fifth mission,

Mission San Luis Obispo de Tolosa, in September of **1772**.

This mission was founded with much less ceremony than generally occurred. Father Serra concluded his official ceremonies there in one day, then returned immediately to San Diego. Only Father Prior Jose Caballer, along with five soldiers and two native converts, remained to carry out the initial construction.

Happily, the natives of the valley proved extremely generous. They supplied the entire missionary entourage with seeds, berries, and venison, and even helped construct a small chapel. The work went slowly at first, but in time a house was built for the resident priest, barracks were constructed, and a granary, kitchen, and shops were added.

The mission facilities grew and prospered, but we must remember they were not originally intended to be permanent settlements. Rather, they were perceived by the Viceroy of New Spain as an advance guard, initial outposts around which towns were to develop. Control of California affairs was to become a secular matter; the primary function of these religious communities was to assure the claim of Spain against intruders from Russia, France, and England.

According to this plan, ten years constituted a sufficient lifespan for the missions. It was understood that at the first opportunity skilled immigrants such as blacksmiths, wheelwrights, and carpenters would follow on the heels of the padres. Thus, before the community of San Luis Obispo had celebrated its first year of existence, Fr. Caballer welcomed to

The New
Community

The Mission
Plan

the valley the first group of Spanish emigrants, including four families.

As priests, soldiers, and settlers learned more about the wilderness that surrounded them, California became less of a mystery. Stories describing the area's resources generated such interest throughout Europe that overtures from other nations soon were directed to the coast. Spain quickly renewed her commitment to the mission project, and on August 19, 1773, Fr. Francisco Palou, the great chronicler of the missions, identified and marked Alta California's southern border. The Dominicans would direct all mission activity south of this point while the Franciscans continued to serve the north.

Seventeen years after the founding of San Luis Obispo, Fr. Jose Caballer, its first priest, died on December 9, 1789. The community continued to enjoy a succession of outstanding leaders.

Perhaps the most engaging of these was Fr. Antonio Martinez, whose career was described in the book *Ramona* by Helen Hunt Jackson. During the tenure of this outspoken padre, secular influences would affect the character of mission life most decidedly.

Fr. Martinez was in truth a generous man — in girth as well as in spirit. Speaking the native language with ease, and counseling with sensitivity and compassion, the padre endeared himself to natives and immigrants alike. All are the

same before God; all were the same before Father Martinez.

That is, *almost* all. Mexican officials stationed in California were not so highly favored in the padre's eyes. In fact, he hated the Mexican occupation; he considered the military administrators incompetent, cruel, and entirely out of their jurisdiction. And, since the fiery padre rarely missed an opportunity to state his opinions, this contempt was widely known; indeed, it came as no surprise to those very officials who had originally approved his appointment to San Luis Obispo. Due to his large following, however, official punishment would have been politically unwise. The solution settled upon, therefore, was to bring false charges against him. During the "trial" that followed, Fr. Martinez was, of course, found guilty and eventually expelled to Spain, but not before his heroic reputation spread throughout California. Stories about hims are legion, the following tale being perhaps the most familiar.

A very young and newly appointed Mexican general named Filipe Moreno successfully charmed his way into polite society, gaining, among other things, a lovely bride thought to be the belle of all California. At Mission Santa Barbara they were united in a most gala wedding celebration attended by representatives from all the missions. After several days of feasting and dancing the young General and his wife departed for Monterey.

En route, Moreno's entourage stopped at each mission along El Camino Real, creating one long, glorious party up the California coast. Each mission prepared the finest foods available, serving their meals in the most festive atmosphere possible. Each mission except one, that is. At San Luis Obispo, Father Martinez didn't give a damn about General Moreno or his new bride. While the more socially-conscious members of his community hurried about making various necessary preparations, the stubborn padre moved among them indifferent to their efforts.

The next day General Moreno arrived standing very tall, but the padre saw only a pompous bore. While the general told of the numerous military and civil courtesies that had been extended to him during his trip, the padre was in pain. As the evening wore on Father Martinez could stand no more, and in the late hours called to his side a group of native friends to help organize what would be his one and only contribution to protocol. Together they planned a formal "pass and review" — an inspection of the troops, a military parade.

The early morning sun had not yet cleared the horizon when Fr. Martinez awakened the General and his bride for this honorary ceremony, and posted them at attention in front of the mission. But before the parade was finally set in motion an unusual and uncomfortable delay occurred. Finally, as the couple stood rigid, the padre marched the entire muster of all the poultry of the mission before them — chickens, ducks, and turkeys arranged according to their size and color. Though the natives struggled to keep them in order, it was mostly an uproar. Thus, Fr. Martinez' version of a military parade.

The Tree As Symbol:
Mission San Francisco de Asis (Dolores)

Fr. Serra slapped his thighs in delight and made a sign of the cross when he learned that a scouting party led by Sergeant Jose Francisco de Ortega had discovered a great bay to the north.

He had particular reason to be pleased. Earlier, when he had complained to the governor that no mission carried the name of St. Francis, the founder of his order, the response

Opposite page: Fragment of Altar Lining

85

had been: *"Si San Francisco quiere mision, que haga se halla su puerto y se le pondra."* ("If St. Francis wants a mission let him show us a harbor and one will be placed there for him.") This newly discovered bay was thus a source of great joy.

Land parties were dispatched to determine the size of the bay, and on August 5th, 1775, Don Juan Manuel de Ayala, commanding the *San Carlos,* sailed through the Golden Gate and made port. Ayala spent forty-four days gathering information and examining the harbor. Upon returning to San Diego he related that while the weather of the great bay was frequently cool and that it suffered occasional heavy fog, there was an abundance of wood and fresh water; and the natives who had greeted him appeared cordial. The building of a settlement was ordered instantly.

Due to the size and location of this great harbor a three-pronged project was undertaken in which, along with the mission, a fort (or "presidio"), as well as a secular town (or "pueblo"), was to be established. Lt. Col. Juan Bautista de Anza, a highly respected trail blazer, was selected to organize and lead a large overland migration to populate these settlements.

Col. de Anza went first to the province of Sonora where he enlisted thirty soldiers with families, and ten single recruits. Twelve civilian families also signed contracts, thereby increasing the total number of persons bound for California to 240. All were given new clothing and their names were added to the Spanish payroll.

Then, in the Mexican town of Tubac the expedition collected horses, mules, cattle, and other provisions. A group of native Mexicans who had been converted also joined the company, as well as several priests, and on October 23rd, 1775, after the singing of Mass, the expedition was underway.

The overland adventures of this group of people tell a story of great hardship and great courage. The story also serves as testimony to the wisdom, thoughtfulness, and skill of Juan Bautista de Anza.

The de Anza
Expedition

Since only one death occurred and several children had been born en route, the expedition arrived in Monterey (by this time a successful mission) in even greater numbers than when they had departed. Here the group divided: some families stayed behind to settle while others continued on to the Bay of St. Francis. This latter group of families, in the company of priests, soldiers and native converts, arrived at their final destination on June 15th, 1776.

The padres at San Francisco Bay immediately directed their attention to the numerous native tribes of the region and set to work on the mission that was to honor the name of St. Francis. Soldiers began construction of the presidio while immigrant families went to work on the pueblo (town). All three facilities — the mission, the presidio, and the civil pueblo — shared the name "San Francisco." But the mission itself was always referred to as Dolores.

On September 15th of each year the feast of Dolores or "Our Lady of Sorrows" is celebrated, recalling the martyrdom

of the spirit as typified most profoundly by Mary, Mother of Jesus. Her statue was quite popular at the mission and very well understood by the native women whose lives had all been touched by the tragedies of an ongoing war between local natives and natives of Contra Costa — "the opposite coast."

On October 9, 1776, the community of Mission San Francisco de Asis dedicated their church. Bells were rung, muskets were fired, the cannons of the *San Carlos* saluted the occasion, and Fr. Francisco Palou sang Mass. Native converts, now members of the community, were among the 150 people gathered for the event. The celebration included a sumptuous feast as well as a procession in which a group of men and boys carried aloft statues of St. Francis and Our Lady of Sorrows.

Like all missions throughout California (and indeed throughout Christendom), the church at Mission San Francisco de Asis, is surmounted by a cross — the central image in mission life. When the communities were first developing, native boys considered it a singular honor to be selected to climb atop the mission for the purpose of affixing this sign. Converts of all ages were taught to regard it in several very particular ways. Each native was invited to understand his or her individual existence as a living experience at the intersection of the cross's horizontal and vertical axes. They were instructed that the longest section of the vertical beam (the part which extends downward from the center) represents each person's ancestors — the tradition from which he came; while the shortest section (the part which extends from the center upward) represents the future — each person's potential, and his or her unity with God. The horizontal beam symbolizes the present living community — the body of Christ. Natives learned that the Christian life is conducted with an awareness of, and a reverence for, the interaction of these aspects. When contemplating the "sacred tree," converts were further urged to recall the life, suffering, death and resurrection cycle of Nature and Jesus.

Analagous to the Christian practice of surmounting the church with a cross, natives, prior to the arrival of the Spaniards, commonly secured evergreen boughs to the apex of their dwellings. The branches were thought to represent the point of absolute beginning. The custom changed somewhat with the coming of the padres, after which converts began to bring healthy young evergreen trees into their mission homes during December of each year. The trees were then festively decorated and given the most prominent positions in the lodge. Natives learned that the function of this gesture was to recall that culture is grounded in nature, and that the tree celebrates the very moment and place of creativity.

The Tree at the Center of the World

"Coyote was walking down the road one day when he noticed that the earth was brown and dry. In the stream-beds there were only dust and rocks. The animals were dying.

"So Coyote walked and walked, up to the top of the mountain to see if he could find the water. He climbed over a ridge, and before him was a lake so large that it contained more water than he could think about. 'What could be keeping this water from running down the hill?' he asked himself. Then he saw that an old man was wedged in the place where the water should run out. The old man was asleep. Coyote went up to him and asked, 'Would you move out of the way so that some of the water can run out?' and the old man said that he would not. Coyote offered him many things if he would move out of the way, but the old man refused. Coyote saw that there was a great tree next to the old man, so he cut it down in such a way that it would fall on the old man and kill him.

"No sooner was the old man dead than a stream burst forth and raced down the mountain. All across the land the water ran. The main part of the stream was wide, like the trunk of a tree, and the creeks were like limbs. All about the stream people came to live. They were like the leaves. And that is the end of this story."

THE SACRED DANCE

Knowing that most things of the world break, Fr. Serra established a set of regulations for all the communities to ensure that mission administration was constant and even-handed. Inherent in these guidelines was a rigid daily routine and style of life.

Dawn came each day with the ringing of the Angelus bell. The women — the wives of the soldiers as well as the native converts — dressed in brightly colored skirts and simple blouses, while shawls were popular protection against the morning chill. Ribbons were dearly prized, and with the slightest excuse the women would also add flowers to their hair. Each native man and boy wore a shirt and trousers which were usually white and generally ill-fitting. Lengths of rope were used as belts, and a serape, or narrow blanket, was *worn over the shoulders. Almost everyone wore a kerchief around his or her neck.*

In an irregular procession the people made their way to morning Mass. Every man, woman and child carried on his or her person a small line of rope which functioned as a record of conduct for the day. Each time a person committed a sin he or she tied a knot in the rope, so that by using different knots and different positions on that line, it was possible at Confession to recall to the padre all sins by kind and number.

After Mass everyone went to breakfast. A homegrown cereal — usually barley — was served; only the sick and aged received milk. Members of the community then went their separate ways, taking up the work of the day until 11 or 12 o'clock when they paused for the midday meal. As this was the largest meal of the day, members enjoyed beef or mutton, and frijoles or cereal. After lunch they rested or attended to personal matters until daily chores were resumed at about 2 o'clock. Sometime during the middle of the afternoon one of the children was assigned the task of providing refreshment for persons engaged in physical labor. A young boy was usually selected to move throughout the mission and the fields, carrying a dipper and bucket of water to which a small amount of vinegar and sweetener had been added.

Most work halted at 5 o'clock, leaving time for the evening meal, entertainment, and religious instruction. Some form of grain cereal was available for dinner, while the industrious referred themselves to their private caches of dried meats, nuts, berries, and/or roasted insects. Families generally dined together, while unmarried adults ate in common.

In addition to a chapel and various commerce facilities (shops for making candles, hemp, etc.), each mission provided separate quarters for the priests as well as the craftsmen and guards. In the long, low wing of rooms attached to the church (the "convento") were two dormitories — one for girls and another for boys. A matron was assigned to each.

The mission design most commonly employed called for the buildings to surround and open onto a court, where members engaged in singing and dancing, and where various types of games were played. This court, actually a garden of small trees, flowering cacti, and other plants, also served as a place for private introspection and meditation.

Within each facility, younger community members learned the necessary skills. Native girls who had converted and were now making their homes at the mission were instructed in the preparation of wool for spinning and in the techniques of weaving, while the boys learned agriculture and a trade. This carefully regulated way of life was enhanced by an essential and all encompassing philosophy.

The people of these communities held existence itself most sacred: life was a "dance." The Royal Road was a promenade where natives, priests, soldiers, horses, and cattle danced in procession. To cut wood was to dance. To make bread and to sing was to dance. The Christians danced in the fields and vineyards. The blacksmiths, the stonecutters, and the weavers danced. The priests danced their sacred processions.

And, of course, nature danced. All around the mission everything expressed this sacred motion — the grass in a light breeze, the leaves of the trees, the trees themselves — all swaying gently.

Mission Bells

Since the typical mission day revolved around such a tight schedule, each facility regulated its activities through the use of bells. Every kind of bell may still be found in the missions: large ones and small ones, bells of metal and bells of wood — all were valued as important gifts to the Church. Though manufactured in a variety of places, some as unlikely as Alaska, most were brought or sent from Mexico or Lima, Peru. Bells tolled the hour and sent people to work. They announced fiestas or were part of solemn service. They signaled the approach of strangers, gave the alarm in case of attack, and reported deaths. And, of course, bells announced the call to worship. Each day closed with *Poor Souls'* bell.

Mission Music

These mission communities "danced" to a babel of other sounds as well, although the use of audible material was so interwoven into the fabric of native existence that a separate, distinct term called "music" very nearly does not obtain. Of course the people had music in the ordinary sense; they had eloquent and sophisticated compositions. But there was also a great plurality of non-compositional sounds associated with life and the living mythology. For example, dancers often imitated the sounds of birds and animals, and made use of a

variety of instruments such as flutes, whistles, rattles, clappers, and drums.

Although the amount of emphasis placed on music varied from community to community, each facility supported a mission choir often composed of more than thirty vocalists who also played guitar, flute, clarinet, and trumpet. Drums, rasps, and rattles accompanied the liturgy, and on occasion the choirs added visual effects to their celebrations by dropping rose petals on the congregation or releasing doves into the crowded church.

In addition, the natives vocalized their prayers, often employing a two-part narrative in which the singer would ask a question and then answer it. Other songs were associated with games, or pertained to hunting, fishing, birth, marriage, and death. Singers and instrumentalists were even asked to perform at secular parties, the most popular being the social dance. These were always gala affairs in which high-spirirted men danced female roles when the women were in short numbers. The musicians performed "men-only" and "women-only" dances as well, and they always accompanied torch-light processions.

Under the direction of the padres the natives became as eager and adept with European instruments as with their own. Hand-crafted guitars and bass violins of a fine quality soon found their way into liturgy or compositions of strictly native origin. Barrel organs — hand crank devices often capable of playing a number of tunes — were next introduced. Some of these could hold a note long enough to be used in conjunction with psalm chants, while others had the ability to render a medley of tunes, some sacred in nature, others frivolous — the popular tunes of the day. To accommodate the musicians and their instruments, lofts were built behind the congregations. From these second story perches the organs and the choir sang out.

Superior skills and achievements in the plastic arts were also brought to mission life by indigenous Americans. The natives were expert carvers of soapstone, sandstone, and wood, using this talent to design and embellish their houses and canoes. For use around the house, objects of great beauty and utility were carved from elk antler, and a wide variety of pottery was produced from the local reddish-brown clay. "Money" was manufactured from highly polished elkhorn or dentalium shells which were held together on strings to ensure easy trading throughout the region.

It was in basketry, however, that the people best expressed their extraordinary gifts — California's carefully woven and coiled containers are still judged second to none. The Pomo, a northern tribe, are particularly noted for the exceptional range in the size of their woven creations. some reach almost four feet across, while others are no bigger than a grain of corn; these served as little gift items. Most Pomo baskets are also decorated with brightly colored feathers, porcupine quills and maidenhair fern. Indeed, throughout California an amazing variety of shapes and styles can be found. One of the design patterns to appear most frequently is a rather simplified row of people holding hands, thus forming an image all the way around the basket. Natives also wove storage and cooking baskets, even sun hats and aprons. "Burden" baskets were manufactured and in common use.

The embellishment of church interiors indicates that California's natives were also excellent draftsmen. In a naturalistic mode they produced individual paintings of subjects such as those indicated by the Stations of the Cross; they also painted directly onto the walls, festooning and embellishing the church interiors. In many ways, these local artists and artisans contributed to their communities both a new understanding of scripture and a significant iconography, making them teachers as well as students in mission life.

Initiation into these developing Christian communities naturally occurred at the baptismal font. In the name of the Father, the Son, and the Holy Spirit, water was poured across the head of the initiate, so that henceforth the convert danced with Jesus, who himself danced on the Cross. To recall the occasion of baptism, holy water fonts — small containers of water — were placed conveniently near the door of each chapel. Converts were instructed to dip their fingers into the font and make the sign of the cross upon entrance to and departure from the church.

Mission life also afforded opportunities to enjoy those other Christian celebrations called "liturgies": first communion, marriage, Requiem, etc. Some liturgies were calendrical, reflecting the cyclical order of nature characterized by life, death, and rebirth. In these, converts paused to reflect upon the God among them, a reality evinced in the community and by all things of which they were a part. They reflected upon the "constant" of creation — that which at once discloses and obscures. And they meditated on the spirit that was maintained in their midst — their communal "body" for the spirit of the Christ.

The notion of a bound community was not introduced to the natives by the Spaniards. At the time of foreign contact indigenous Californians had long been living in small tribal settlements often referred to as *rancherias*. The differences among these native communities — their values and their aspiratons — came forward in obvious ways. Disagreements between villages led occasionally to bloody combat, but more frequently problems were resolved, and differences expressed, during athletic events. Using a ball made of hide and stuffed with deer hair the natives played a form of soccer — a rough-and-tumble contest usually held in a neutral valley with both communities present to cheer their teams.

Considerable emphasis was placed on the internal security and well-being of each single community, with proper conduct and social order being maintained through the performance of correct rituals and the sharing of resources. Natives fished and hunted together, always dividing the catch; when an individual learned of a hungry friend he customarily tightened his own belt.

Community membership was therefore not without responsibility. By learning and following the "Good Way," both the individual and the community succeeded. This meant that members were to heed the advice of elders, and to "dance" to a multiplicity of rules and regulations.

———————————

"Coyote was walking down the road one day, thinking only of food. It had been several days since he had last eaten and he felt so sorry for himself that he sobbed with his face against his arm. His stomach was making noises like boiling water and his head hurt. And then, near where the sumac grows, he saw great clusters of red, delicious-looking berries! Coyote grew very excited as he ran over to grab them. Just as his hand touched the berries his mind remembered a talk he had had with the Wise Old Man. During one of their many conversations Coyote had asked, 'Tell me, Old Man, where did we get this land; was it given to us by our ancestors?' And the Wise Old Man replied, 'Of course not, Coyote. We are borrowing this land from our great, great, great, great grandchildren. We must take good care of it because it belongs to them. To remind us of this, the children of the future have put bunches of red berries near where the sumac grows. These berries are theirs, so no matter how hungry you get you must never eat them. They are only to remind you that the land belongs to the children yet to come.'

" 'What will happen to us, Old Man, if we do eat the berries?' asked Coyote. And the Wise Old Man replied, 'I am sorry, Coyote, but if you eat the berries your ass will fall off.'

"This is what Coyote rememberd as his hands touched the berries. He stopped and thought a moment. Sweat was running down his face, and he said to himself, 'I have always known that the Wise Old Man is a fool! What does he know? He is just trying to keep the berries for himself. Besides, how could I owe something to people who are not even here yet?' So Coyote ate the berries. He ate as fast as he could and he ate as many as he could. Coyote felt fine! He looked behind him and his ass had not fallen off. He laughed very loudly and began skipping down the road.

"He had not gone far when his stomach began to hurt something awful. And then he began to get diarrhea, first a little, then a great stream. Coyote was sick, the sickest he had ever been! Coyote felt terrible! He thought about the children who were yet to come, and he thought about the Wise Old Man, and he was very embarrassed. Coyote walked slowly to the river where he got a drink of water and then he went to hide himself in the deep bushes. He didn't want anyone to know that he had forgotten the children yet to come, and that his ass had fallen off! And that is the end of this story."

Silent Vestiges of the Dance:
Mission San Juan Capistrano

The mission of San Juan Capistrano, unique in a number of ways, was founded twice.

When it was first decided that a facility should be established to divide the travel between San Diego and San Gabriel, a padre was assigned from each of the missions — Father Fermin Lasuen of San Diego, and Father Gregorio

Opposite page:
*Sanctus (Holy)
Bell*

109

21 SAN FRANCISCO DE SOLANO
20 SAN RAFAEL ARCANGEL
6 SAN FRANCISCO DE ASIS
14 SAN JOSE
8 SANTA CLARA
12 SANTA CRUZ
15 SAN JUAN BAUTISTA
2 SAN CARLOS BORROMEO DE CARMELO
13 NUESTRA SENORA DE LA SOLEDAD
3 SAN ANTONIO DE PADUA
16 SAN MIGUEL ARCANGEL
5 SAN LUIS OBISPO DE TOLOSA
11 LA PURISIMA CONCEPCION
19 SANTA INES
10 SANTA BARBARA
9 SAN BUENAVENTURA
17 SAN FERNANDO REY DE ESPANA
4 SAN GABRIEL ARCANGEL
7 SAN JUAN CAPISTRANO
18 SAN LUIS REY DE FRANCIA
1 SAN DIEGO DE ALCALA

Amurrio of San Gabriel. They identified support people — both natives and soldiers — and laid in stores for the trip. Fr. Lasuen left San Diego with his small company in October of 1775 and proceeded north on foot, staying near the beach as much as possible, since a dense fog filled the lowlands. The image of these silent men must have been not unlike a Japanese brush painting of figures wading in mist — sometimes emerging, sometimes disappearing altogether.

Fr. Amurrio descended from San Gabriel, and upon reaching their destination, both he and Fr. Lasuen were more than satisfied with the location. Nearby Trabuco and San Juan Creeks provided plenty of fresh water, and the ocean itself lay less than three miles away. Also, substantial limestone deposits for use in the making of mortar were available at El Torro Quarry, and an abundance of building stones could be found in Trabuco canyon. With irrigation, the soil, too, would prove satisfactory.

Local natives received the missionaries well. The padres presented gifts to the natives, shared food, and the curious and friendly among them soon assisted in construction of a temporary stick-and-branch structure called a "ramada." Everyone joined in the founding ceremony: together they planted and blessed the cross, mounted bells on the limb of a tree, and celebrated Mass.

These occasions were intentionally made festive by the padres — the ringing of the bells, the sharing of the food, the celebration of the Mass — all culminated in a heightened

The Mission is Founded

110

expression that formed the basis for the new, shared community.

Yet these people, the constituents of the new community, had no sooner cleared the way for the first permanent buildings than a messenger arrived from San Diego telling of the attack in which Father Jayme had been killed. Not knowing if this was a general uprising of all the tribes in the Southland or if hostilities had been localized in San Diego, the padres became more than uneasy. Since it was also unclear whether local natives were aware of the incident (and, if not, how they would react when they received the news), the padres hastily buried their bells, made a present to the natives of all the goods and supplies, and the entire company jumped onto the backs of pack mules and executed a hurried retreat to San Diego. When they came into sight of that mission, Fr. Serra, relieved at their safety, called for the church bells to be rung in Thanksgiving.

It was a year before the effort was taken up again.

In the meantime, Fr. Serra appointed Fr. Lasuen (his heir-apparent) as senior official at San Diego, while he himself assumed the task of starting anew at San Juan Capistrano. He traveled to the area in the company of Fr. Amurrio and Fr. Pablo Mugartegui. Together the three priests located the still intact cross that had been constructed the previous year, unearthed the bells, and prepared an altar. Then, on November 1, 1776, the Father-President celebrated — for the second time — a formal founding ceremony in honor of the

14th century Italian theologian, St. John of Capistrano. He then returned to San Diego, leaving the mission in the care of the two priests and a handful of soldiers.

The natives were not at all displeased with the return of the padres. They cut timber, and, directed by drawings on ledger paper and sketches made with a stick in the dirt, constructed first a chapel and then houses. In a short time the gardens of San Juan Capistrano produced in abundance. Fruit trees — peaches, apricots, and pomegranates — were planted, and fresh vegetable grew in abundance. They also cultivated grapes, utilizing a local variety of grape as well as vines which Fr. Serra had brought with him on his original voyage from Mexico.

Though he was not able to get there often, Mission San Juan Capistrano was a favorite of Fr. Serra. He occasionally officiated at confirmations in the chapel that now bears his name, cherishing the opportunity to sing Mass and celebrate baptisms in this small building which is claimed to be among the oldest in California.

As of 1785 over 500 baptisms had been entered on the mission roll and more than 400 native converts were making their homes at San Juan Capistrano. One hundred burials and 125 weddings had also occurred.

Within ten years the mission barracks and a series of shops for industry had been constructed. Granaries were built, and forty tiny houses were in use. All of these structures, including the palisade which surrounded them, were made from adobe bricks — each brick measuring twelve inches wide, four inches thick, and twenty-two inches long.

On February 2, 1797 (22 years after the first founding), construction of the "Great Church" began. Designed in the form of a Roman Cross, this splendid edifice eventually measured 180 feet in length by 18 feet in width, and bore an arched roof crowned by seven domes and topped with a high bell tower that could be seen from miles away. It was a monumental accomplishment. Members of the community — men, women, and children — carried stones from a canyon six miles away, while sycamore logs used in making rafters and beams were delivered from a nearby canyon. The walls of the facility, though of varying dimensions, were in some places as much as seven feet thick. With its spacious and lofty interior this new church was truly the "jewel" of the missions. It had taken its members nine years to build it.

A gala consecration was held on September 7, 1806, attended by the padres, the military governor with his entourage, and members of other communities. Amid music and dancing and the waving of banners onlookers could observe that the presidio soldiers had put on their formal dress uniforms for the occasion.

Six years and three months later (December 8, 1812), the "Great Church" was in ruins.

On that particular December morning, the weather was hot and sultry. More than sixty members of the community, mostly natives, were making their way to Mass when, suddenly, the ground began to sway. Two young boys charged with ringing the bells cried out as the tower fell, and before the trembling stopped the entire building was in rubble, never to be rebuilt. Fifty natives were buried, including the two children.

The earthquake of 1812 was not the only misfortune that struck Mission San Juan Capistrano. There was a series of tragedies throughout its history. In 1806, the year that the "Great Church" was consecrated, native converts were subjected to first one disease then another, imported by the Europeans. Since they had developed no immunity against such infections, over 130 died from measles and an equal number succumbed to smallpox. In later years, the mission community suffered destruction or loss by mice, insects, and fire. Floods, too, advanced to destroy the buildings while salt deposits left by receding waters wasted the soil.

Then, in December of 1818, two ships commanded by the pirate Hyppolite de Bouchard were seen anchored in the harbor three miles away. In an effort to thwart the imminent raid, a messenger was sent to San Diego, and the presidio commander there promptly dispatched thirty soldiers to protect the northern facility. By the time they arrived, Bouchard had already drafted a most courteous message to the mission demanding that certain goods and supplies be delivered to the beach. The community, realizing that Bouchard was in a position to wipe them out entirely if he so desired, was ready to negotiate. But, to their consternation, the commander of the armed detachment, Alferez Arguello, sent word that "Captain Bouchard could go to hell!" The pirates then made their move, charging from the beach yelling and screaming, flashing swords and firing muskets for psychological effect. However, Bouchard and his men apparently placed no greater emphasis on physical training than they did on integrity. The two-and-one-half-mile run from the beach proved so fatiguing that when the attackers arrived at the mission in a position to fight, they dropped to the ground exhausted. Under cover of chaparral, these daring sea-dogs spent the first forty minutes of battle catching their breath.

The soldiers meanwhile had posted themselves on a small rise suitable for sustained fighting. Unfortunately, though their location provided more than adequate protection for themselves, it was really too far away to protect the mission. Bouchard's men laid sack — they took everything they wanted and burned several of the buildings to boot.

The Mission
is Sacked

Of course, the mission survived these tragedies in one form or another, and it can be visited today. But it is perhaps the implied eloquence of things past that most moves a visitor. Particularly moving are the remaining ruins of the "Great Church." Also at Capistrano is a series of tunnels sometimes compared to the catacombs of the early Christians. This maze of underground corridors was most likely dug by members of the community under direction of the padres, but the date

115

they were dug, and their reason for being, is still uncertain. While many have been closed by cave-ins, it is clear that at one time they constituted an elaborate network.

Some historians have speculated that during the period of Mexican occupation the missions were eyed covetously, causing the community at San Juan Capistrano to move its considerable wealth underground. Other explanations suggest that the tunnels were merely escape routes, though the discovery of resting mats and furniture seems to indicate that they were inhabited by a number of people for a substantial length of time.

A no less compelling account suggests that Mission San Juan Capistrano was the site of a masterfully designed irrigation system embracing literally thousands of acres. The project must have included cisterns, reservoirs and masonry aqueducts. Aboveground there would have been miles of *zanjas* — adobe and stone-lined ditches — by which water could be carried to the mission and the fields.

Today San Juan Capistrano is the most generous of all the missions — it is open and spacious, relaxed and unfettered. The birds and animals walk around freely on the grounds, and perhaps humans feel that this hospitality extends to them as well.

The mission's ambassadors are, of course, the swallows. There are stories about them, songs about them, and tourists gather by the thousands each year to watch them return from their annual migration. In the cracks and crevices, and on the flat mission walls, they build round mud nests. San Juan Capistrano is their home. They dance in from the direction of the sea, routinely arriving on the 19th of March, as if determined to be home on St. Josephs Day. Like the mission itself, they too are a legend.

———————

The Dance of the Church:
Mission Santa Clara de Asis

St. Clare was born in the year 1193 in the same town as St. Francis. She spent her youth much as any other girl of means until about the age of nineteen, when she first heard Francis preach. Clare was deeply moved by the experience, and soon thereafter entered the convent of Portiuncula, where she was later joined by her mother and sister. Aided by

Oposite page:
St. Clare

119

Francis, she then established and provided leadership for a "Second Order" which now bears her name, its members commonly referred to as the *Poor Clares*. These women chose to take the same vow as their male counterparts, the Franciscans: chastity, poverty, and obedience. (Later, regularly employed laymen sharing similar vows were organized into a "Third Order.")

St. Clare was a gifted missionary and a most capable administrator. Yet while her life soon became a model of piety, obedience, and devotion to work, she is also remembered as an exemplar of wit, charm, and beauty. Less than three years after her death in 1253, Clare was canonized.

On November 28th, 1774, Father Francisco Palou arrived at a location south of the "Great San Francisco Bay" that was to become the first of several sites upon which the first of many churches would be erected. Each was dedicated to, and placed in the custody of, Madre Serifica — Santa Clara de Asis.

Actually, Father Palou's visit to the South Bay was only preliminary. Though he did select the site and plant a cross, another site was later chosen in honor of St. Clare, and the mission itself was officially founded January 12th, 1777. But because of heavy rains and flooding, the new community was forced to move.

Securing a new site, they began what seemed to be an endless series of church-building. The first two church buildings were made of logs, not uncommon in original mission architecture. The population grew, and on November

19, 1781, Fr. Serra laid the cornerstone for a third, more permanent chapel. The community worked for three years on their new church, painting it gaily and proudly placing the saints in their proper niches. When it was completed, Fr. Serra returned to celebrate its formal dedication. (It is interesting to note that the Father-President's cornerstone was recovered in later years during an excavation. Carved into the fifteen by twelve by seven inch stone was a three and one-half inch square pocket containing a bronze crucifix and a number of coins — the most recent dated 1768 — carefully wrapped in an oiled hide.)

In 1812, Santa Clara's church suffered a fate similar to that of other churches at other missions: its walls were fatally weakened by powerful tremors in the earth. Another quake in 1818 destroyed the building completely. Although a new site was selected and a new church dedicated in 1822, this church, too, was destroyed. The community never seemed to be free from having their major energies expended in church construction. But, they were tenacious, and yet another church was built.

In 1851 the mission itself was transferred to Jesuit leadership and a college was established on the grounds. As the entire facility was soon surrounded by campus buildings, its new chapel eventually became the spiritual center of the University of Santa Clara. Still, the "nine lives" of this church were not yet over. In 1861 the structure was remodeled, and in 1926 it was razed by fire. University faculty and students rushed in to save numerous relics from the flames, one of which — the "All Souls" Bell — had been customarily rung each evening at 8:30. After the fire a group of engineering students hastily erected a scaffolding from which to suspend this valuable object, originally a gift from the King of Spain. The bell still pealed nightly, without interruption.

Despite the seemingly endless difficulties of the Church, Mission Santa Clara de Asis at its height enjoyed numerous successes. It surpassed, or at least equalled all other facilities in several ways: in agricultural production and number of conversions it was outstanding; its ranches maintained over 5,000 head of cattle plus 12,000 sheep; and its converts achieved impressive results in their shops, excelling in spinning and weaving; in making candles, wine and brandy; and in other household arts.

Early in the life of Mission Santa Clara a civil pueblo was founded near the grounds. However, it was not long before the settlers (many sent by officials in Mexico to form a settlement there) so encroached upon the mission that native converts were pushed off their mission lands. The padres responded by insisting upon a legal survey. When completed, the investigation called for all lands appropriated by civilians to be returned to the natives. Although the mission community won the day on this particular point, relationships between the mission community and the pueblo became further estranged, with the civilians harrassing the natives and in general making life as difficult as possible for all concerned. It was Father Catala, one of the two resident priests, who came up with an idea that helped bridge the gap between the pueblo and the mission. As a gesture of friendship, the natives of the community planted three rows of trees that formed a wide, willow-lined avenue between the mission chapel and the town, and presented it as a gift to the pueblo. Town members could dress in their Sunday best, as befitting this festival promenade, and travel the four miles to and from the chapel. This road linking the communities — "The Alameda" — still remains as the central thoroughfare in Santa Clara.

Since the Santa Clara mission became part of a Jesuit college in 1851, the present church there, completed in 1929, is perhaps more reflective of the Victorian style of the other campus buildings than of mission architecture. Some critics feel that, compared to the authentic style, the present chapel appears conspicuous — more pious than powerful, a bit of the prude.

Still it must be remembered that if major construction decisions had been made locally at other sites, these churches too might have been built much differently — certainly they would have been less modest. As things worked out, however, building expenditures were carefully watched in Mexico City. Since military authorities controlled the purse strings, it was expected that plans and budgets would be submitted and approved well in advance of construction, and that nothing "lavish" would be built.

The word "Church" itself falls upon ears primed with preconceptions, resonating by way of multiplicity of meaning. The term can refer either to the hierarchy of officials or to the universal religion. It can describe the specific place of liturgy as well as the body, or membership, invested in a particular community. The notion of "Church" as a reference to community, as opposed to the notion of church as a structure, is underpinned and substantiated by a review of language. The Greek word *Ecclesia* gave the French *eglise*, which was applied to those who had "come together." For Hellenized Jews *ecclesia* came to mean the community of Christians. While the tight relationship that later evolved between the *faithful* and the *building* may be contrary to the wishes of the authors of Christianity, it, too, is a notion of long-standing.

As the Christian community understands Communion to be the high point of a spiritual awakening that begins with baptism, the church is also thought a particularly appropriate place for the taking of this sacrament. One or more altars or tables are therefore conspicuous in each mission chapel. (It should be noted that the tradition of referring to altars as "tables" is not to disparage the usual understanding of an altar, it is rather to indicate that in the Christian community an ordinary household table is an altar before God.) It was at these tables that communities shared the sacred feast — the Eucharist. Mindful of this most central celebration, the Franciscan padres followed European conventions when designing California's churches. Particularly they imitated the Roman model, an east-west oriented structure in which they built the "apse" (a vaulted recess) at the end of the *nave* (the church's principal room). The altar itself was placed in the recess and elevated by at least a few steps. A rail was added to define this sanctuary.

In Europe, each of the great churches had been built over the burial place of a saint, and the altar itself was contructed over the actual grave. Since this was not possible in the mission, the priests instead mounted into the altar a large stone from which a plug was removed and a relic of a saint inserted.

The Altar Stone

Of all the buildings that constituted a Californian mission, the church with its lofty cross remains the most imposing. The wings off the sides of a chapel — the "conventos" — are generally enhanced by colonnades and joined by semicircular arches along the sidewalks on the patio side. The conventos were rarely more than a single story in height.

The "campanile," or bell tower, can be found in a variety of arrangements. Sometimes it is incorporated into the facade so that the bells are high and conspicuous from the front of the building, but occasionally the bells themselves are placed in windows or openings in a solid wall. At Asistencia San Antonio de Pala the companile is free-standing — separated altogether from the church.

The Bell Towers

As protection against earthquakes, massive tapered buttresses reinforce either side of church exteriors. The beams and rafters, even the bells, were fastened by lengths of rawhide.

Throughout the Christian world the egg-shaped dome has been incorporated into church architecture, and the missions are no exception. But consensus is that of all the appointments in mission churches, the pulpits are particularly captivating. They are found in a variety of designs, the most engaging and joyous being those fastened to the wall high above the floor, looking not unlike elegant bird cages. Some of the mission communities designed and constructed sounding boards, canopies, which occupy the space above the heads of the preachers. Although they also provide visual highlights including painted designs of the heavens and a carved white dove (the Holy Spirit) suspended by a wire, the primary function of these canopies is to amplify the spoken "word." While the pulpits themselves were actually made of wood, a "fool the eye" coloring technique gave them the appearance of marble.

The wall beyond the table, originally considered a part of the altar, is called the "reredos." This wall contains niches or windows to accommodate the saints, thereby contributing significantly to the joy and celebration of the church. In some missions these walls are also painted; in others the entire surfaces are charged with gold. As backgrounds for the corpus they establish the dramatic point of focus for the tension between God the Father and the community — the Dance of the Church.

126

Crucifix,
polychromed wood,
Circa, late 18th cent., Philippines

The Covenant and the Canoe:

Mission San Buenaventura

Seventy-one miles north of Los Angeles on El Camino Real stands the 9th Franciscan facility established in California. Mission San Buenaventura is one of three coastal communities (the others being Santa Barbara and La Purisima Concepcion) discretely sheltered by the Santa Barbara channel islands.

According to Fr. Serra's original plan San Buenaventura was to be the third mission founded, but only after twelve

21 SAN FRANCISCO DE SOLANO
20 SAN RAFAEL ARCANGEL
6 SAN FRANCISCO DE ASIS
14 SAN JOSE
8 SANTA CLARA
12 SANTA CRUZ
15 SAN JUAN BAUTISTA
2 SAN CARLOS BORROMEO DE CARMELO
13 NUESTRA SENORA DE LA SOLEDAD
3 SÁN ANTONIO DE PADUA
16 SAN MIGUEL ARCANGEL
5 SAN LUIS OBISPO DE TOLOSA
11 LA PURISIMA CONCEPCION
19 SANTA INES
10 SANTA BARBARA
9 SAN BUENAVENTURA
17 SAN FERNANDO REY DE ESPANA
4 SAN GABRIEL ARCANGEL
7 SAN JUAN CAPISTRANO
18a SAN ANTONIO DE PALA
18 SAN LUIS REY DE FRANCIA
1 SAN DIEGO DE ALCALA

The New Community

130

years of frustration and delay did the Father-President receive approval to commence construction. Finally, on March 6th, 1782, the famous padre left San Gabriel under the personal protection of military governor Felipe de Neve and his staff. The party was also accompanied by a group of natives, by Fathers Francisco Dumetz and Vincente de Santia Maria, and by seventy officers and soldiers with their families. It was a high-spirited and carefree procession that danced away from the protection of Mission San Gabriel to found a new facility.

Pausing at numerous native communities en route, Fr. Serra eagerly explained to the tribal leaders his intention to build a mission among them. He described the buildings that would be constructed, the nature of the community that would evolve, and how the natives might participate. A less genuine man could scarcely afford to telegraph so completely his intentions.

When the expedition arrived at the native community of Zucu, Father Serra, now nearly 70 years old, founded his last mission. It was Easter morning, 1782, thirteen years after the founding of the first mission in San Diego. After the expedition pitched its tents among the trees, Fr. Serra called all of the company about him, as well as those natives who were willing to listen. He spoke of the resurrection of Nature and of the Christ, and dedicated the mission to God in the name of those human values exemplified by St. Bonaventura — the Serific Doctor, friend of St. Thomas Aquinas. A large cross was planted firmly in the ground.

In all aspects of their lives, the people of Zucu — the Chumash — looked toward the ocean. Their homes, conical huts of willow construction, as well as their industry, economy, and interests were directed toward the Pacific waters. The Chumash were fishermen and boat-builders, and their art of carving was highly developed and broadly applied. Although all their wooden utensils were beautifully worked and functional, the many splendidly carved boats were particularly conspicuous. Fishing vessels were manufactured from pine boards doweled or tied together, and canoes were formed from single logs. The boats were painted, incised, carved in deep relief and decorated with bold designs that spoke of the qualities of the sea and of its relationship with the people. The Chumash were excellent sailors. Spanish observers reported that nowhere in the world had they seen small boats move at such incredible speeds, nor had they otherwise observed canoes so far out into the open sea.

Like all native Californians, the people of Zucu were highly developed in their concept of family life. Priests at several mission locations complained that natives never restrained or punished their children, which was in fact, true. If it became absolutely necessary to reprimand a child, the task was carried out by someone else, usually an uncle. Fathers and mothers maintained, exclusively, a relationship of support, comfort, and love. That parents did not pamper children who became ill seems at first to contradict this concept, but it is apparent that the natives took issue with a common practice

131

in other cultures, that is, they were careful to avoid rewarding sick children with gifts and special attention. Illness was not a condition for which children might receive a reward.

In general, the tradition to which the California native danced must be characterized as one of *covenant* rather than *law*. A covenant relationship is one which maintains both a vertical and horizontal tension, meaning that individuals respond to the dictates of their own consciences (which had themselves been forged in the community) as well as to the ordinary constraints of a social life. In order for an individual to remain in good standing with his group — it was expected that he would live in obedience with what were believed to be his or her own true promptings — a vertical relationship with the divine. Thus, existence was experienced as a tension, with the horizontal mediating the vertical, and the vertical mediating the horizontal. The result proved to be a generous world view; the natives respected and honored a great diversity of personal ministery; no contribution was insignificant. In this way the covenant served the whole, and, perhaps, served it with greater equity than might be realized under a system of law.

Christianity, too, reflected this tension. It was, in fact, in many ways consistent with essential native values. Many of the Chumash embraced the new faith and worked cooperatively beside the padres. The natives dug irrigation ditches, planted fields, and cultivated garden vegetables, even succeeding with the more exotic plants such as pomegranates, bananas, coconuts, sugar cane, figs, and plaintain. Before this new community could enjoy its recent bounty, however, a fire destroyed all of the buildings.

By 1801 construction of a new church began. Natives carried materials from a broad area — timber was cut from trees at Santa Ana and Ojai, while a beautiful altar and paintings were delivered from Mexico. The community then built a raised pulpit and manufactured tiles for the floor. Though the church was finally dedicated in 1809, within three years it suffered considerable damage again, this time as a result of the earthquake of 1812. The tower and part of the facade were immediately rebuilt, and total reconstruction was completed in 1816.

With the passing of time, converts at Mission San Buenaventura collected about them certain articles — metal knives, cooking utensils, clothing, etc. — of great value to the non-Christian natives. From throughout the region natives arrived requesting the opportunity to trade for these items. The exchange of products soon became a regular practice — usually good fun — though at times arguments grew heated and tempers flared, causing violent fights and bloodshed.

A desire to trade prompted twenty-five Mojaves to travel from the Colorado River area to the mission in 1819. While loitering about the grounds, their behavior apparently became rude and rowdy. Mission soldiers came forward to restrain them and eventually locked them in the guardhouse overnight. During the early hours of the morning one of the Mojave natives created a clamor and demanded to be released. A guard struck him.

Outraged, the other prisoners began breaking up furniture and insisting that they be freed. The two guards who entered the cell to quiet them were clubbed to death. The Mojaves then escaped. An alarm was sounded, and soldiers turned out in force as the weaponless natives made their way to the edge of the compound. When they got to the palisade and were beginning to help each other over the top, the soldiers appeared, ready with muskets. Ten of the natives were shot; the remainder cleared the wall.

The soldiers quickly organized a manhunt in which all who had escaped were recaptured and taken to the nearest presidio, enslaved, and forced to toil in chains. Fearing reprisal from other Mojaves of the Colorado River, the mission was carefully guarded for some time.

Church "Modernization"

The destiny of this community is perhaps reflected in the ultimate destiny of the church building itself. Though it retained the authentic character of mission architecture until 1893. a resident priest decided that the church, then serving the city of Ventura, should become "modern." He removed the Mexican altar and tore out the pulpit, painted over the native murals and added dark stained glass windows. The beam ceiling was covered with tongue and groove boards and wood was placed over the tile floor.

In 1957 the church was rescued from this remodeling and returned as nearly as possible to its original state. In some instances, happily, "modernization" had protected the original structures.

The Ventura Chamber of Commerce later added a bronze tablet to the large cross on the hill behind the city. On it were inscribed these words:

> "In memory of the 200th anniversary of the birth of Padre Junipero Serra, founder of the Franciscan Missions of California, who closed the labors of his useful life with the founding of the Mission of San Buenaventura, March 31, 1782, this tablet is placed."

Fr. Serra

Fr. Serra died two years after completing his work at San Buenaventura, on August 28, 1784, in the company of his colleagues at Carmelo. Just prior to his death the Father-President advised the priests to "do with me as you will." In the European tradition, they buried him in the sanctuary of the old adobe church at Carmelo. The present church is on the same site, and his grave may be seen in the sanctuary there today.

———————

The Dance of Solitude:

Mission Santa Barbara

When Junipero Serra died, Fr. Fermin Lasuen was ultimately chosen to assume the responsibilities of Father-President. Under his capable leadership nine more missions were founded. The first was Santa Barbara.

The area of the Pacific coast protected by the channel islands was perhaps the most densely populated part of   137

California at the time of Spanish contact. There were twenty villages in the area of present-day Santa Barbara alone. Since Father Serra had originally planned to build several missions in this region, three of which were to be served by a single presidio, it naturally fell upon Father Lasuen later to implement the plan. Thus, during his first year in office the new Father-President made the trip to El Pedragoso, as the area was known by the Spaniards. A presidio had been established here four years earlier (Fr. Serra was in attendance at the founding ceremony), and upon his arrival Fr. Lasuen found it complete, well-manned, and secure. He therefore planted a cross almost within the shadow of this garrison on Dec. 4, 1786. Twelve days later the mission in honor of St. Barbara was officially dedicated, and Mass was sung.

By the middle of January, construction of a new church was well underway. The first church was made from green wood and was quite modest; however, a more substantial version (42 by 15 feet) was completed within a year. Seven buildings of adobe construction followed, and by 1788 clay tiles roofed them all. The extraordinary number of converts associated with this mission soon made it necessary to enlarge the existing chapel, and finally to erect a new and much larger church altogether. This new building measured 125 feet by 25 feet.

To accommodate the rapidly increasing Christian community, a "mission village" was established in which

The New
Community

138

individual family units were constructed by and for the natives. As at other missions, an adobe palisade 9 feet in height and 3,600 feet in length was also erected. Tiles were attached to the top of this structure in an effort to integrate the wall with the architecture of the church. Tiles also protected the palisade itself from washing away.

Santa Barbara quickly became popular with immigrants. By 1807, 252 individual dwellings dotted the streets of the town. But like so many others, this mission, too, suffered greatly from the disaster of 1812. On Monday, December 21st, as the community awaited Christmas, the powerful quake struck. Violent tremors along the San Andreas fault damaged the mission church beyond repair.

At Santa Barbara and elsewhere, an ingenious technique was sometimes employed in church reconstruction which might have been learned by watching certain clever insects. Any ruin that remained sturdy was used as the basic scaffolding for future construction, so that the new building was erected along the outside of the remains of the old. When this new structure was complete, the ruins that had been trapped inside were broken down and carried out the front door in small pieces. The new church would be larger, and human bodies interred beneath the floor of the old church would not have to be disturbed. In this fashion, the community of Mission Santa Barbara constructed a church 170 feet long and 40 feet wide. The walls, which measure six feet in thickness, are supported by buttresses of nine by nine

The Town
of
Santa
Barbara

The Earthquake
of
1812

Construction
Techniques

feet. Two twenty-foot-square towers of solid stone and cement, one of which contains a passageway to the roof of the church, flank its facade.

The New
Church

Upon completion of the church, a gala dedication was held, including music and fireworks. After the celebration, the interior of the church was finished with a shiny cement floor made from lime and oil, and furnished with statues of Santa Barbara, the Purisima, and San Jose. Small sculptures of St. Dominic and St. Francis also captured the eyes of visitors.

There were, however, no pews in the church at Santa Barbara. There were, in fact, no pews in any of the early Franciscan missions. Instead, patrons provided their own seating: children sat on the floor, boys on one side and girls on the other; senior citizens brought stools; and the rest of the community used mats, usually of dried tule. Some of the young women vied with one another in making little rugs decorated with embroidery.

Bouchard
Lands

Santa Barbara was also among the many missions "visited" by the pirate Bouchard. In November of 1818, aware that four of his men were being detained at the presidio as a result of an earlier skirmish, Bouchard directed a representative to negotiate an exchange of prisoners. A quick head count at the fort revealed that nine soldiers were absent, and the presidio commander, assuming that Bouchard had them, negotiated a trade. A time and place for the exchange was selected: at night on a point close to the beach. Exactly as specified, the presidio commander released his prisoners, but there was a

short delay before a lone figure stumbled out of the dark from the direction of Bouchard's ship. The man, the pirates' only prisoner, was immediately identified as a local thief and drunk, of whom the town of Santa Barbara had been trying to rid itself for many years.

The geographic location of this mission proved in many ways a blessing. The surrounding region, characterized by a Mediterranean climate, enjoys a very happy combination of moisture and dryness, so that stormy interruptions in the continuity of long, sun-filled days are rare. This fortunate place, therefore, had always had a dense population. This fact did not change. However, as more and more Spaniards came into the town, more and more natives were deprived of their land. So while the population never fell, it underwent a dramatic shift in profile.

The Lady of Solitude

There is a story that involves a different kind of population shift, the famous story of the solitary lady of San Nicholas Isle.

In April of 1835, according to the official record, a chartered schooner, hired to accomplish two quite separate tasks, sailed out of the Santa Barbara harbor. First, the crew conducted a three month otter hunt on the channel islands. Then, by direction of the padres, the Captain set sail to a point well beyond the other channel islands to locate and safely deliver to mission Santa Barbara all native residents of tiny San Nicolas Isle.

During this expedition a great storm came up, forcing the

schooner to anchor several hundred yards out from the island while part of the crew went ashore in small boats. As conditions were risky, the boat crews were indeed fortunate to reach land. The natives hastily and confusedly collected their valuables while giant swells and violent winds jeopardized the schooner. Once on board the schooner, a certain native woman discovered that her child was missing and became frantic, pleading to be returned to the island. The sailors tried to convince her that sending another boat into the rough sea would be impossible, but agreed to return on the next day or at first calm water. The woman objected that her child might then be lost, and in an instant jumped over the side and disappeared into the foam.

The crew hastily delivered all other islanders to Santa Barbara mission and explained the situation to the padres. Though everyone intended to go back as soon as possible, one delay succeeded another, and within a month the schooner capsized in a storm and was lost.

There followed a period of time during which no other ships large enough to make such a long trip on the open seas were available, and soon the story was generally forgotten. However, it was *not* forgotten by the mission's resident priest, Fr. Gonzales. Yet despite the offer of a reward nothing was done. Finally, almost sixteen years later, a ship did become available. At Fr. Gonzales' urgings a search party set out immediately, only to return with reports that not a trace of living humanity might be found on the island. Even if the 143 woman had succeeded in gaining the shore, she was presumably dead by this time.

Eventually, various other stories about distant San Nicolas were heard in Santa Barbara. Among them, reports concerning the island's large population of seal and otter generated the greatest interest. Hunting parties were organized, and for the duration of a month they scoured the island killing otter by the thousands.

One stormy evening during this expedition, a sailor thought he saw a figure on a rise at the head of the island some distance away. But by the time he was able to gain the attention of the other men the figure, or apparition, was gone. This incident engendered numerous tales of the Ghost of San Nicolas Island.

A second expedition of hunters was eventually organized, and in 1853, a third. It was during this latter trip that someone identified in the sand the small slender footprint of a woman. Preliminary speculations gave way to the inevitable conclusion: the woman abandoned here 18 years before remained alive.

The three-by-six mile island would obviously require a detailed search. The entire area was therefore broken into a grid and individuals were assigned to the various sectors. They discovered a brush hut, a fire pit, and various additional signs of habitation, but they could find no person. Thus the search was discontinued and the men went back to work.

Then fresh footprints were seen. Determined to find the

mysterious resident, the expedition spread out again, this time with attention to the rocky, cave-filled side of the island. Perhaps she knew the men were there and was watching — simply too frightened to come forward.

Finally one of the sailors saw her. Creeping up to avoid signaling his presence, he confronted a handsome woman, forty or fifty years of age, in apparently excellent health. She wore a long dress made of bird feathers.

Native members of the rescue party tried to communicate with her in various dialects, but she could neither understand nor be understood by any of them. Eventually, through gestures, the woman realized that she was to go away with them, and quietly packed the objects that had served her during this long exile. She then walked to the boat carrying a fire brand, as she must have done on her island treks so many times before.

The woman was taken across the channel and delivered to Fr. Gonzales, who arranged for her to be the permanent guest of Mr. and Mrs. George Nidiver, local Catholic residents. The people of Santa Barbara found the woman a great curiosity, and some even requested to include her as an exhibition in a traveling show. But the lady of the island received many thoughtful visitors, too. Members of the community frequently brought her gifts which, though graciously received by this modest and gentle woman, were in turn presented to children.

As time passed, various aspects of her life on the island emerged. She had, of course, been successful in her swim from the schooner to the island. But her search for the child literally yielded only bits and pieces: her baby had been eaten by wild dogs. She lived on fish and birds which she captured in a snare, and also on cabbages and edible roots. She made tools for cooking and sewing and constructed several dwellings, though she spent most of her nights in a cave on the north end of the island. In such fashion, she was able to stay reasonably comfortable during her time of solitude.

Juana
Maria

Yet this bright and curious woman, who had survived so well on the island, grew ill within a few months in civilization. The Nidiver family tried to nurse her, finally even duplicated the foods she ate on the island. When she lacked the strength to walk, she was carried each day to a chair in the sun. But nothing worked. The Nidivers sent for the padres to minister to her, and she was baptised "Juana Maria."

On September 8th, 1853, the lady of solitude died. She was interred in the cemetery of Mission Santa Barbara.

*Opposite page:
"Yellow pitaya"—
a cactus flower.*

Toward a Christian Education:

Mission La Purisima Concepcion

La Purisima is located in a picturesque glen almost halfway between Santa Barbara and San Luis Obispo. Unlike the typical mission model, it is a long and narrow facility, and is the most complete and carefully restored mission in California today.

The road to this mission, as to all the missions, is marked

Opposite page:
La Purisima
Concepcion

149

with bells erected by the El Camino Real Association, a California organization specifically charged with the task of placing markers to designate the famous "Royal Road." Metal posts eleven feet in height are set in cement and curved like shepherds' crooks at the top, each holding a one-hundred pound bell from its tip. The bells were each cast with two dates on them: 1769, the year that the first mission was founded, and 1906, the year that the marker project began. The first bell was erected at the Plaza Church in Los Angeles on August 15th. Upon a signal, a cannon was fired and the bells of every Catholic church in Los Angeles simultaneously announced the event.

In 1906, membership in the El Camino Real Association required dues of $2.00 per year which were used to make and mount the bells. While the initial fifty-four bells were placed only to the south of Santa Barbara, interest in the project soon developed in the north as well. San Francisco erected ten bells at mile intervals along the Royal Road, and other areas quickly responded. Twenty-four more bells were erected, then two hundred and fifty, then four hundred. San Diego County mounted a bell per mile, while Orange County provided ten bells, and Ventura, San Mateo and Alameda counties came up with slightly less than one bell per mile. Santa Barbara County also became enthusiastic about the project and mounted a sizable number of bells, among them the one at Mission La Purisima Concepcion.

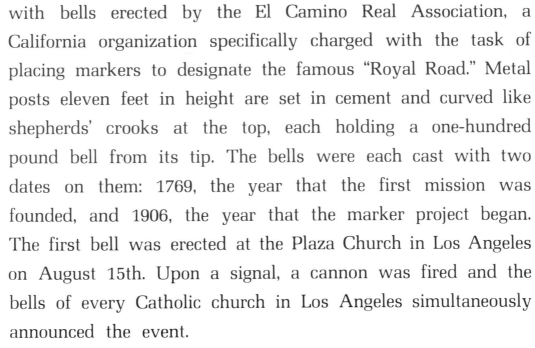

21 SAN FRANCISCO DE SOLANO
20 SAN RAFAEL ARCANGEL
6 SAN FRANCISCO DE ASIS
14 SAN JOSE
8 SANTA CLARA
12 SANTA CRUZ
15 SAN JUAN BAUTISTA
2 SAN CARLOS BORROMEO DE CARMELO
13 NUESTRA SENORA DE LA SOLEDAD
3 SAN ANTONIO DE PADUA
16 SAN MIGUEL ARCANGEL
5 SAN LUIS OBISPO DE TOLOSA
11 LA PURISIMA CONCEPCION
19 SANTA INES
10 SANTA BARBARA
9 SAN BUENAVENTURA
17 SAN FERNANDO REY DE ESPANA
4 SAN GABRIEL ARCANGEL
7 SAN JUAN CAPISTRANO
18a SAN ANTONIO DE PALA
18 SAN LUIS REY DE FRANCIA
1 SAN DIEGO DE ALCALA

This was the eleventh mission, and Mary, Mother of Jesus,

was chosen as its exemplar (La Purisima Concepcion de Maria Santisima — "The Immaculate Conception of Mary the Most Pure). Its founding date was December 8, 1787. Rain poured down as Father-President Lasuen planted the Cross, blessed the site, and sang Mass. Throughout January and February — well into March in fact — the deluge continued and the soggy earth delayed construction until April. By August, however, seventy-nine natives had joined the community and the mission made rapid gains. Every man, woman and child from the more than fifty native villages in the area was finally baptized into the Christian community.

Unfortunately, the first church was hastily erected and collapsed within twelve years. Then, in 1802, a fine building of adobe construction with the characteristic tile roof was dedicated, and the native converts built over a hundred small adobe houses for themselves. Along with shops and gardens, the community was quite complete.

Disaster struck in the form of the great quake of 1812. Within four minutes of the first rumblings of the earth, every building at La Purisima Concepcion was badly cracked and torn. Then, the hill behind the mission opened and a great flood of water and black sand boiled out of the earth. The entire mission was gone; even the orchards were wasted.

The community was forced to begin anew. Another site was chosen about five miles away across the river, in what was known as "The Valley of the Watercress." The padres immediately requested permission to build a new church, and good progress was made until 1816, when a winter drought destroyed most of the animals. Then, in 1818, a fire took several buildings, including all of the converts' homes. The members of La Purisima Concepcion made another beginning. This time the community experienced frost damage; and the fields were destroyed by swarms of locust, the granaries by squirrels. The mission would suffer other fires, floods, earthquakes, and drought.

Despite these hardships, La Purisima still managed to become a highly successful community. At one time the members maintained 1,000 horses and over 13,000 sheep and cattle. San Gabriel and Santa Ines were the only communities which developed more bountiful gardens. Also at La Purisima Concepcion, 3,400 souls were baptised and over 1,000 marriages celebrated.

However, a mere recital of statistics cannot portray the quality of interchange that occurred between the two cultures — Spanish and Native American — nor did conversion occur by happenstance.

Throughout California, the Franciscan missionaries made use of a tightly packaged system — a well-formulated strategy for the conversion of natives. This technique, designed at the Franciscan headquarters in Mexico and field-tested in Texas and the Sierra Gorda, was the one used at La Purisima. The first step toward "educating, reforming, or uplifting" a human being was to provide for his "reasonable comfort and safety." The Franciscans were instructed to make presents of food and clothing, always to be gentle, and to count on their most routine chores at a new site to pique the native curiosity. They were urged to invite native participation when clearing the land, and to seek help in constructing the first rude huts. Natives were asked to induce their friends to join in the work, and every assistance was rewarded. Regular meals were shared with all. These were the first steps toward a Christian education.

The converts were also encouraged to make their homes close to the mission — at first in huts, then in comfortable, whitewashed adobe homes. Single men and women were kept carefully separate, spending their nights behind locked doors. Young people anxious to change this situation could do so by getting married. In this process, presented in an over-simplified manner, a man petitioned the priest with his request to marry and the padre then introduced him to the girl of his choice. The girl was free to reject the suitor or make plans for her wedding. When the latter occurred, banns were published, the marriage was celebrated, and the young couple was soon situated in their new adobe home. Henceforth they attended mass and religious instruction together.

The children of the mission were initially taught the liturgical calendar — those days of special Christian significance. They learned to show respect — to genuflect (bend the knee) and make the Sign of the Cross. In groups and with tutors, boys and girls mastered rote learning

Religious Instruction

exercises as well as the Spanish names for Jesus, the Holy Trinity, and the Saints.

But the natives were in no way coerced into conversion. Indeed, they could *not* share in Communion until they had committed to memory the Lord's Prayer, the Hail Mary, and the Creed, the Confiteor, the Act of Contrition, the Acts of Faith, Hope and Charity, the Ten Commandments, the Precepts of the Church, the Seven Sacraments, the Six Necessary Points of Faith, and the Four Last Things.

The catechumen was also carefully directed. Each native participated in processions and became familiar with the lives of the Saints and with pictures of Heaven and Hell. Converts learned the Stations of the Cross and were taught the significance of Communion and the Eucharist. Though religious instruction in the missions was part of a daily routine, major holidays were particularly exciting occasions for learning. Community members dressed in costumes to re-enact major Christian themes and events, the most popular of these being conducted during the Christmas season.

Such was the pattern of religious life in La Purisima, a peaceful pattern shared with other missions, just as they all shared a pattern of battling natural and man-made calamities in order to survive.

But at La Purisima, it was secularization that finally "killed" the community, bringing to a close the initial chapter in the story of this mission. The buildings abandoned, nature began the steady process of returning them to the earth.

At the turn of the century the site was visited by writer Helen Hunt Jackson, who reported that most of the structures were in ruin. The roof of the church was broken and rags hung from the ceiling. Windows and doors were gone, the altar rail was down (as was the pulpit), and piles of trash were everywhere. The church was now the home of various birds and animals; the other buildings were overgrown with weeds.

The property came to be owned by Union Oil Co. of California, and finally by the State. In the early 1930's, the National Park Service sought the advice of various consultants to determine if the mission could be restored; and engineers, archeologists, and architects soon arrived at the scene. A very young Harry Downie (the man who was later to become master builder and architect of the mission restoration), participated in this, the most ambitious project of its kind ever to take place in the West.

After poking about the site for a year, experts concluded their research and prepared extensive drawings. The young men of the Civilian Conservation Corps arrived in 1934, and, meticulously employing the same tools and techniques that the natives had used, they rebuilt the entire facility under the leadership of the National Park Service. When the work was completed, the mission became a State Historical Monument.

La Purisima Concepcion, located near Lompoc, California, is "dancing" still. Across an open field stretches the long mission complex. Conspicuous are the cross, the campanario, and the tiled palisade. The shops and the priests' rooms are complete, and the tannery is at a polite distance.

The grass dances at Mission La Purisima Concepcion, as do the flag and the trees. Visitors move down the walkway and in and out of rooms along the colonnade — they too particpate in the sacred dance of life.

———————————

THE SACRED FEAST

For many years a sense of personal unworthiness was impressed upon Roman Catholics. For example, the church dictated that no follower should participate in Communion without elaborate preparation — certainly not without Confession. Today this has changed, and even the most bucolic of bishops acknowledge that *forgiveness* is implicit in returning to the table of one's loving father.

Before the coming of the Spaniards, the natives had their own concept of inherent transgressions: they, too, believed in "original sin." What this specifically meant to the native mind was that man, *unlike* anything else in nature, is capable of making a mistake. This does not mean that we shall inevitably err, but only that we have the capacity to do so. Man is born imperfect.

The solution perceived by the natives was to learn the rules of nature and to live in obedience to them. Anything contrary to the "Good Way" could be highly destructive to an individual or to the entire group. Thus, if the village suffered a disaster — a disease, flood, or earthquake — it was believed to be the result of some personal transgression. It then became necessary for the person responsible to "turn around," to go back to the order of nature. The community, reflecting the boundless love of the Great Spirit, honored the transgressor's renewed covenant and was obliged to forgive repentant individuals of all their sins.

The native custom of assigning a meaning, or value, to the delicate order of nature gave rise to considerable misunderstanding among Spanish settlers. In time of drought, for instance, occasional groups of natives moved throughout the region offering to make rain — generally for a fee. Though always treated suspiciously, "rainmakers" were very much in demand.

The natives themselves understood that when nature is balanced it *will* rain: it's supposed to. A lack of rain revealed that someone in the settlement had acted contrary to the natural order. Therefore, as part of the rainmaking process, natives camped near the town for a few days to observe the scene, trying to determine if the community had identified the fault and if the citizens had turned back around to the "Good Way." When they believed that this had occurred, they began their celebration by dancing and singing. Their chants could be translated:

> "When Nature is balanced it does rain. We celebrate this; we are singing. When Nature is balanced it does rain. We celebrate this; we are dancing. We are in balance with Nature; we are singing. We are dancing — it shall rain."

Though their successes were mixed, it rained more often than not. When it didn't, the rainmakers were declared failures and driven away as charlatans. The natives themselves left with no sense of personal loss, however, being content that the covenant of the community remained broken, therefore it couldn't possibly rain.

When natives first joined a mission church they were instructed that in becoming Christians, they were joining an ancient community. Truly, they annexed history. In the evening, after the fields were tended and the cattle fed, the new Christians came together, sitting on the ground in the patio to hear the padres tell stories of places far from California. The converts learned of Egypt, Mesopotamia, and Syria, and of a group of migrant workers, very low in the caste system, who spent their lives wandering. Though these nomads actually lived in Egypt, they knew no "state" boundaries. They were nationless, traveling with their families and their few belongings like gypsies. As a result, they regularly functioned at the edge of law, often outside of it.

The Habiru

161

As individual nomads occasionally withdrew to join the mainstream of society and others simply disappeared altogether, the membership of the group was in constant flux. Collectively, the wanderers who traveled with their flocks and took advantage of the seasons and pastures were called the Apiru, or Habiru — the Hebrews. The mission padres spoke of the many crucial events in their lives: their oppression, their Exodus, and their covenant.

Christian communities in California thought of these early Hebrews — their precursors — as a single group of people who suffered and celebrated the whole range of human experience. The Hebrews were the first people to record their history — orally, and then on paper. They described their wanderings, their political problems, and the wisdom that they gained. They wrote love poems and mythical explanations of their origin. They called their god "Yahweh." Finally, those who followed Christ wrote of the reformer who came among them, and of the complexities and joys of the event.

The natives of California took up, and were taken up by, many aspects of this ancient tradition. Particularly they embraced one of its central elements of celebration — the feast. However, while converts shared the ordinary Hebrew meal of bread and wine, the event itself was actually experienced in the missions symbolically, since only very small amounts of these substances were served. During such celebrations the mission communities recalled together certain aspects of their history and related these past events to occurrences of the day.

The responsibility for this special feast, including the preparation and serving of the meal, fell to the padres; small metal presses which had been brought from Spain during the very first days of mission development were used in preparing the host. These resembled long-handled scissors which in place of cutting blades contained round metal discs that pressed together as the handles were closed. The two discs were also engraved on the inside surfaces, so that when a piece of soft bread was placed between them and pressure applied, a round wafer with designs on either side was produced. Serving as the Eucharist, large numbers of these flat breads were broken for the meal.

Throughout the mission period, representations of the pelican appeared in banners and paintings as symbols of the sacred feast. The mother pelican, when unable to provide food for her children, pecks her own chest until she draws blood, and with this substance, nourishes and sustains her family. Even today, the pelican image is an appropriate emblem of this sacred Christian celebration.

The Feast of Fools:

Mission Santa Cruz

On September 25, 1791, near a splendid stream called the San Lorenzo River, a mission to honor the Sacred Cross was founded. The Commandante of the San Francisco presidio, Don Hermenegildo Sal, ceremoniously laid claim to the land, after which Father Salazar sang Mass. The site had been chosen and blessed by Father Lasuen the month before.

165

21 SAN FRANCISCO DE SOLANO
20 SAN RAFAEL ARCANGEL
6 SAN FRANCISCO DE ASIS
14 SAN JOSE
8 SANTA CLARA
12 SANTA CRUZ
15 SAN JUAN BAUTISTA
2 SAN CARLOS BORROMEO DE CARMELO
13 NUESTRA SENORA DE LA SOLEDAD
3 SAN ANTONIO DE PADUA
16 SAN MIGUEL ARCANGEL
5 SAN LUIS OBISPO DE TOLOSA
11 LA PURISIMA CONCEPCION
19 SANTA INES
10 SANTA BARBARA
9 SAN BUENAVENTURA
17 SAN FERNANDO REY DE ESPANA
4 SAN GABRIEL ARCANGEL
7 SAN JUAN CAPISTRANO
18a SAN ANTONIO DE PALA
18 SAN LUIS REY DE FRANCIA
1 SAN DIEGO DE ALCALA

The New Community

The cooperation of the local natives was quite beyond belief. They immediately set to work unloading and constructing, assisting in every way. The padres later learned, however, that this was all part of a clever scheme. The natives, worldly by now from hearing of other missions and aware of the possibilities that existed, were stealing about half of what they touched! Meanwhile, Sugert, the tribal leader responsible for the scheme, stood at the padre's boot with all his followers, awaiting only the next opportunity to serve. He himself insisted on being the first tribal candidate for baptism, while Commandante Sal agreed to serve as his godfather.

This was a different California than when Fr. Serra first arrived here, and exchanges between Spaniards and native Americans were never again to have quite the same quality of trust as before.

Nonetheless, together these new friends burned the grass and marked off sites where various structures would stand. For themselves, the natives built huts nearby.

Actual construction was delayed, however. As was often the case, supplies promised by the government in Mexico were not delivered on time. However, Fr. Salazar obtained loans and gifts from other missions and went on as best he could. Carmelo presented to the new community six horses and mules, while Santa Clara offered 22 horses, 64 head of cattle, 770 pounds of wheat grain, and 26 loaves of bread. Mission Dolores contributed two bushels of barley, 70 sheep, and five yoke of oxen. Tools were also loaned by other missions.

The facility itself was constructed near a dense forest close to the bay. As in other communities, **a** church was erected, this one measuring 25 feet in height, 30 feet in width, and 112 feet in length. It stood on a three-foot stone foundation and enjoyed a facade of masonry. The natives built and quickly put to use a grist mill and the usual service buildings.

The Church

Santa Cruz was also a location chosen by the government as a site for a civil community. Three such settlements of "pueblos" were eventually established within the chain of mission communities: Los Angeles, San Jose, and the community at Santa Cruz, named Branciforte in honor of the Marquis de Branciforte, Viceroy of Mexico. To establish a settlement, Comisionado Moraga arrived on the scene, surveyed the area, and selected a site just across the San Lorenzo River. A young consulting engineer named Alberto de Cordoba was then commissioned to organize the new town. He had irrigation ditches partly dug and the construction of temporary dwellings underway, when settlers from Guadalajara arrived on May 12, 1797.

Branciforte

The pueblo was comprised, by the most generous description, of a motley collection of immigrants. None of them had originally wanted to settle the new pueblo, but as their only alternative was to spend time in a Mexican prison, the thought of exile at Branciforte grew more and more appealing. This unique group of settlers consisted almost entirely of thieves, cutthroats, gamblers and prostitutes. Thus

The Citizens

it is not suprising that, soon after their arrival, the town became a haven and hideout for criminals from all California. And, as corrupt city officials channeled all city improvement funds to their own personal accounts, Branciforte remained a village of shacks.

The new settlers soon established a number of public houses devoted to liquor, prostitution, and every conceivable gambling technique. And, strangely enough, Branciforte became particularly noted for its Saturday night *spider races*; large sums of money changed hands as the small creatures crawled or spun to victory.

Like the Franciscans, these Brancifortians also attempted to include the local natives in all their activities. But obviously, the Fathers of Mission Santa Cruz were in no way pleased with the idea. Padre Olbes — one of the resident priests — did all he could to discourage their sinful practices by writing letters to the city fathers and attempting to counsel the town through the pulpit. The Brancifortians responded to his attempt to project authority by electing an unofficial mayor to represent them: his name was Moses Grosz.

There was only speculation as to where Mr. Grosz had come from, but it was believed that he had spent time on the Eastern frontier in the region of Tennessee or Kentucky. He had certainly been a church-goer at some point in his past, albeit not a Catholic one — his absent-minded singing of Protestant hymns in a monotone and off-key voice proved singularly annoying to Father Olbes.

Immediately prior to making his home at Branciforte, Grosz had been "self-employed." Everyone knew that he supported his large family by providing the ships of San Francisco harbor with fresh poultry, although the source of his endless supply of chickens and turkeys remains a mystery.

Moses Grosz had seven children by a large, homely woman — a virago whose first name has been lost to the past, though for some reason at Branciforte she was addressed as "Flower" (an unlikely name for the only person on earth whom Moses Grosz ever feared). It was an ordinary Branciforte rumor that Mrs. Grosz, aided by her sewing shears and Moses' drunken sleep, committed something like a circumcision upon him. Several witnesses testified that on another occasion, "Flower" smashed her husband across the face with the back of his guitar while he was napping in a chair!

Despite intimidations by his wife, the citizens of Branciforte generally acknowledged that Moses Grosz was a formidable man, though in fact he had already entered the middle stages of alcohol deterioration. The costume in which he was constantly seen — the one in which he was buried — included boots, jeans, a dark wool shirt, and a leather jacket, the sleeves of which had long ago rotted off to the elbows. His face was always stubbled with what appeared to be a seven-day growth. Following his appointment as Mayor, however, Moses added to his wardrobe a tall black hat — the "stovepipe" later made famous by Abraham Lincoln.

At one point, Fr. Olbes was reduced to seeking the mayor's assistance. During the Christmas season of 1818, the ships of Hyppolite de Bouchard were reportedly seen off the northern coast headed for Santa Cruz. Knowing that Bouchard would not hesitate to kill anyone who stood in his way, Padre Olbes led the mission community inland to safety. First, however, he had to ask Mayor Grosz and the citizens of Branciforte to protect the mission in his absence.

The prevailing winds changed, and Bouchard's ships could not land at Santa Cruz. But Mayor Grosz, a man who kept a wolf and chickens in the same barnyard, nonetheless led an expedition to the deserted mission. Though we don't know all that transpired, reports prove that the visitors drank the wine and brandy, carried away supplies in great quantities, and helped themselves to personal belongings. Their conduct inside the church was particularly inappropriate.

Upon his return to the mission Father Olbes screamed with rage, declaring that the Brancifortians had "desecrated the church," and "stolen everything that could possibly be carried away." He begged his superiors for permission to "desist and abandon the mission." Permission was denied, but the superiors did conduct an investigation. One young woman was found wearing an item identified as being stolen from Padres Olbes' personal trunk. That item was a pair of ladies' hose! Charges and counter-charges flew back and forth, but nothing was resolved.

In 1840 the roof tiles of the chapel were carried off by

native children after a tidal wave felled the tower. And the mission lands were slowly embraced by the town of Branciforte. The church walls came down in 1851 and vandals destroyed the remainder. The mission completely disappeared.

At present, a scale replica of the Old Mission Church stands at Emmet and School Streets, built in commemoration by the citizens of Santa Cruz in 1931.

———————————

A Community in Retreat:

Mission Nuestra Senora de la Soledad

When the salmon spawning season would arrive, California's natives came together beside fresh water streams to enjoy the bounty of the rivers. These were indeed festive occasions. In accordance with tradition, a person of great respect was selected to take the first salmon of the year, and as the natives gathered to examine it, speculations about the

173

coming season were offered. The fish was then cooked with considerable ceremony while stories of other "first" salmon were passed around — what the portents had indicated, and what had come to pass. After the fish was cooked, it was divided into as many pieces as there were people; a feast of communion and thanksgiving was thus shared by the entire community. When the meal was over, young native men tumbled into the water to fish in earnest, sweeping the catch high up onto the bank with their hands.

Other sacred feasts took place in the inland valley. There, natives gathered together in front of a large fire and waited for the wood to be reduced to coals. They then spread out and formed a circle several hundred yards in diameter, and began to move slowly toward the coals, singing, dancing, and striking the ground with sticks, thus driving hundreds of grasshoppers before them. At the center the dancers confronted a mound of roasted insects. Having a flavor similar to that of nuts, the grasshoppers were either eaten by the handful like popcorn or ground and added to other dishes. Like the salmon, they constituted an important food supply, and were central to celebrations of thanksgiving for fellowship and God's plenty.

It was in the Salinas Valley, where such festivals were held, that Father-President Lasuen chose a mission site in early 1791. Though the region itself was dry and dusty, the padre was able to locate a spot that offered pasture when it rained and promised gardens if irrigated. At this place known

to the few natives residents as *Chuttusgelis*, the Father-President planted a cross and began the journey home.

On October 9th of the same year, in the company of two priests, four soldiers and six natives, the padre returned to dedicate the site. It was a hot and barren place, and the quiet of the valley was only occasionally interrupted by the wind. In this lonely and desolate region, the "unlucky" thirteenth mission was founded and quite appropriately dedicated to Nuestra Senora de la Soledad — "Our Lady of Solitude." The small party hastily constructed a straw-roofed adobe church which they named the Chapel of Soledad.

As there were few natives living in the surrounding area, progress was slow on every front; during the first year the padres were joined by fewer than a dozen converts. Nonetheless, this small community managed a tile roof for its church and a long, tiled convento. Their most monumental achievement was the impressive aqueduct that carried water to the mission.

The New Community

Soledad slowly came into its own, but it was never among the most productive of the missions. Still, at the high point of its success, 700 natives belonged to the community, and the mission maintained over 4,000 head of cattle and almost 5,000 sheep. It was excellent agricultural country, and for every 25 bushels of barley sown, the yield was 120. With great success the community grew horse peas, Spanish peas, Indian corn, Indian beans, and wheat.

Mission Productivity

Unfortunately, Mission Nuestra Senora de la Soledad

experienced setbacks as well. Flash floods destroyed the church in 1824 and 1828, and before the building could be wholly reconstructed it was lost again to an earthquake in 1832. A series of epidemics claimed the lives of many converts; rheumatism and lung disease afflicted the missionaries. Furthermore, the mission quarters were so dark and damp that the priests often suffered from depression and asked to be reassigned; some thirty padres passed through during its early years.

Fr. Florencio Ibanez

In fact, the mission's only permanent resident priest was Florencio Ibanez. Fr. Ibanez was a trusted friend of the Spanish governor Jose de Arrillaga, and when the Spanish governor took seriously ill in later years, he requested to be taken to the isolated mission and placed in the padre's custody. Though Fr. Ibanez was unable to effect a cure, he did carry out his companion's final request; the governor was dressed in a Franciscan robe and buried in the mission churchyard. Padre Ibanez was himself later interred at Soledad; he was the only priest to be buried there.

Because of its inland location, Mission Nuestra Senora Dolorisimi de la Soledad (as it was called by the community) routinely functioned as a place of asylum. According to church law, each mission enjoyed this Right of Asylum — an ancient practice following Moses' provision that "*he who is forced to flee for manslaughter, may have at hand whither to escape.*" Thus, individuals sought for crimes large or small could take themselves to a mission for protection. The point was not to shield criminals, but to guard the rights of the accused, making certain each had a fair trial and thus avoiding hasty executions. In practice this meant that officials could remove no one from the custody of the priests without written assurance that a fair and impartial trial would follow. Officers of the law who violated the rule would be excommunicated — expelled from the church. The Spanish officers therefore generally honored the right of asylum.

Of the many stories told about Mission Soledad's role as a retreat, the tale of Father Vicente Francisco de Sarria is perhaps the most poignant:

During the period of Mexican occupation, the government officials near Soledad and throughout California became rather nervous about Catholic opinion or Catholic bias, and, of course, the "Catholic vote." Several governors honestly believed that Catholics shared a common opinion on all matters, and should therefore be held suspect; while in fact mission members commonly expressed a variety of political opinions.

It was this misunderstanding that so severely affected the career of Vicente Francisco de Sarria. Padre Sarria was a bright, bookish man whose convincing arguments did, in fact, hold sway over many people — Catholics and non-Catholics alike. Though reserved by nature, Fr. Sarria took firm exception to the injustices of the Mexican regime, and to make matters worse, he refused to sign a document pledging his allegiance to that government. The outspoken padre nonetheless rose to power within the church hierarchy. He

177

functioned as *Commisario perfecto* and, for a brief period, as Father-President of the missions. But because of his candid, unsolicited opinions of the government, he was constantly intimidated and harassed by the law.

Finally, under threat of exile, Fr. Sarria removed himself to Mission Soledad, where he remained during the decline of the community. Poor conditions had made it difficult to maintain cattle, and the high disease rate did not help attract natives. In 1834 the Franciscan officials at Carmelo learned that Fr. Sarria was practically alone at Soledad; only a few other members of the community remained, and the padre himself was weak from exhaustion and starvation.

In May of 1835, while celebrating Mass, Fr. Sarria fell before the altar. Upon his death that same day, the natives carried the body of their priest to Mission San Antonio de Padua for burial. They then dispersed, never to return to Soledad.

Opposite page:
Cylindropuntia—
a cactus. ("Cholla").

Poverty, Prosperity and the Paradox:
Mission San Jose

The establishment of permanent civil "pueblos," or towns, was originally the plan of Governor Felipe de Neve; it was he at any rate who ordered settlement of the three that concern the mission story: Branciforte, which has been discussed in some detail; Nuestra Senora la Reina de los Angeles de Porciuncula, now abbreviated to Los Angeles; and San Jose de

Guadalupe, where Mission San Jose would be built. (Mission San Jose was unique in that there was a secular community near the site when it was founded.)

In the initial stages of secular development, every possible inducement was used by the Spanish government to bring settlers to these outposts. Each was alloted an annual salary for five years — approximately $115.00 for the first two, and $60.00 for the last three. Families were also provided with starter livestock and farm implements — as well as a separate lot on which to construct a house — and were even granted the right to pasture on government lands. Settlers paid no taxes for five years, though they were expected in return to donate any agricultural surplus to the nearest fort, and if called upon, to function as members of the military "ready reserve."

Each pueblo was given about ten square miles of land on which a quadrangular plaza was built, either at the center of the parcel of land or on a waterfront. Surrounding and facing the plaza were public buildings, usually consisting of a courthouse, a jail, stables, shops, a bar or two, and storage facilities. In time, a firehouse and postal facilities would be added, and the church was generally erected nearby. Merchants and civic leaders in search of housing sites bartered over any remaining lots. These plazas quickly became the informal social centers of the secular communities. Cockfights and bullfights were held here, and on occasion someone would wrestle a bear.

In addition to a town council, an *alcalde*, was appointed to each community. Though these officials often patronized those who came to them with problems, they were in the main good men; citizens generally received fair verdicts during routine criminal cases in which the alcades served as judges. Beyond a silver-headed cane and the prestige of the office, there was no salary or reward associated with this position.

The civil pueblo of San Jose was founded on November 29, 1776, on the banks of the Guadalupe River, though it took ten years for the settlers to gain legal possession of the land. It was still comprised of only a few random shacks eleven years after that, when the padres arrived to establish a mission.

Mission development had been interrupted for several years, after Santa Cruz and Soledad were founded in 1791. But the advantages of establishing additional facilities in time became apparent: a fairly continuous chain of missions would make traveling more convenient and secure, would discourage settlers from other parts of the world, and in general would make them stronger in collective resources.

After the practice of founding new missions was resumed, authorization was given for the development of five new facilities. The first site chosen was located next to the foothills southeast of San Francisco Bay; on the other side of the bay, Mission Dolores could be seen on a clear day. A small party planted a cross near Alameda Creek, and on June 11th, 1797, Father-President Lasuen sang Mass and dedicated the mission to Joseph, husband of Mary.

The New
Community

By December a tule-roofed wooden church had been completed, irrigation ditches had been dug, and temporary outbuildings were being used as shops and granaries. Thirty-three new Christians joined the community.

Mission San Jose was located fifteen miles from San Jose pueblo on El Camino Real. Fathers Isidoro Barcenilla and Augustin Merino were placed in charge, aided by 12 yoke of oxen, 12 mules, 39 horses, 240 sheep, and 60 pigs.

San Jose quickly became one of the most expansive facilities; by 1824 almost 2,000 natives were making their homes here, a number which ranked the mission second only to San Luis Rey in terms of population. The padres married 1,984 couples and welcomed 6,800 souls into the Christian community. Later the mission functioned as a boarding school for orphaned children who, under the watchful eyes of Dominican sisters, played among its famous, shielding olive trees.

As time passed, however, a series of conflicts developed at San Jose. In January of 1805, a native woman appeared at the mission requesting that the padres minister to a relative who had taken ill in a village fifteen miles away. Fr. Cueva responded, and in the company of three soldiers and four native converts, set out for the rancheria. Once the party was away from the protection of the mission, a group of natives hostile to the idea of a mission being imposed in their midst fell upon them and killed three converts, one soldier, and all of the horses. Fr. Cueva himself received head injuries.

Soldiers of the San Francisco presidio and settlers from San Jose pueblo quickly formed a posse. The natives left a broad, east-bound trail and were soon overtaken. In the skirmish that followed eleven hostiles were killed. When the remainder were captured, it was discovered that the entire band was composed of women!

This was not the only group that resented the presence of the mission. Their cause was later taken up by a gifted young native named Estanislao. Estanislao had spent his youth in Mission San Jose, where he had moved about so quietly that his unusual talents might have remained a secret were it not for his superior intelligence and ease in learning. However, the mission reality, whatever its virtures, was not for him. Upon reaching adulthood, the young man rebelled against the constraints of mission life, longing for the existence he had experienced before the coming of the Spaniards. With his companion and lieutenant, Cipriano, and a numerically strong cadre, this charismatic leader unceremoniously left the mission community in 1827. He was later joined by a number of women and children and the band returned to the "old ways."

Estanislao

Military detachments were sent after Estanislao and his band, but to no avail. He conducted daring daylight raids on civil pueblos, stealing horses and other goods needed to support the growing number of followers.

In terms of prowess, bravery, and knowledge of military strategy, the name Estanislao has become associated with such legendary warriors as Dull Knife, Crazy Horse, and

185

Cochise. And, like those others, Estanislao was also deemed a magician. Reports came to the presidio that he and his men had been seen in several places simultaneously, but when sought by military detachments, they were no place to be found.

At length the military devoted their major energies to the capture of this powerful leader. But when mounted campaigns went out against him, often only odd soldiers straggled back to the presidio. It was General M. G. Vallejo, Commander-In-Chief of the California militia, who finally assembled the force that would bring him in. Advised of the band's whereabouts, the General and his troops crossed the San Joaquin River to surround a wooded camp. The soldiers then set fire to the forest in an effort to burn the group out, and several of the rebels finally appeared at the edge of the flaming woods in search of fresh air. Silhouetted against the smoke, they were easy targets.

Under cover of darkness, Vallejo sent a squad of twenty-five men into the smoldering forest. Three of these men were wounded, however, and they returned within half an hour. At dawn, the General himself and forty men entered the woods. Meeting no opposition they advanced to find only abandoned barricades. Estanislao was gone.

Vallejo regrouped his men, and within a week the detachment gained another opportunity to surround the natives. The soldiers cut a trail with *machetes*, installed a cannon, and made a complete circular wall of aimed rifles.

The general petitioned Estanislao to surrender, but the native leader announced that his people preferred "the quick death of a bullet to the slow death of civilization." As if by one shot, all of the natives except three women were dead.

Because of the uncompromising pursuit of his vision, the name Estanislao soon became synonymous with "integrity." To hold this magnificent warrior in their collective memory, the people of California named *Stanislaus County* and the *Stanislaus River* in his honor.

At mission San Jose and indeed throughout California, the land was conducive to both the raising of cattle and the grazing of sheep, and these two economic enterprises grew during this period. Some ranchers, including those on the large mission lands, successfully maintained both types of stock. However, as the grazing habits of cattle were truly more polite, the majority of cattleman detested both sheep and shepherds. The ability to keep these animals separate was one of the numerous advantages to owning large parcels of land.

For political reasons, Spain made a series of generous allotments to favorite loyal citizens, and in 1775, Mr. Manuel Butron received the first of such grants, thereby establishing himself as California's first independent rancher. During the Mexican occupation the land grant policy was very liberal. Any Mexican could request up to "eleven square leagues," though many ranchos were much larger (a ranch of 4,500 acres was not out of the ordinary). With the exception of

Land
Grants

187

territory already occupied by native communities, pueblos, and missions, the recipients of these grants were free to take any parcel of land that appealed to them.

The method used to identify the new ranches began with a natural marker, such as a stream. Ranchers then determined the size of their holdings by dragging a fifty foot line along a boundary and marking the corners with piles of rocks or the skulls of cattle.

The Ranchos

In 1790 roughly twenty ranchos had been established. By 1830 California was the home of more than fifty land barons, and by 1850 a million-and-a-quarter cattle were being tended. Beef and beef by-products sustained the economy of the region, and the large steak soon became the most prestigious dinner entree. Sheep were sometimes used for mutton, but were more often prized for their thick wool. This was woven into blankets or serge cloth by native women.

In addition to the great ranchos, vegetable and crop farms were developed in both secular and religious communities. A heavy tree limb was often used as a plow. Wheat was planted in square mile furrows and was later cut by hand and bound in sheaves. Native women winnowed the wheat by placing it in shallow baskets and throwing it into the air to separate the chaff from the grain. Finally, the grain was processed by the hooves of horses.

Secular Feasts

Though the people of the ranchos entertained themselves and their guests in a variety of ways, the most popular celebration was undoubtedly the *fiesta*. The whole of a beef was roasted over a great hot bed, while chickens and turkeys were tucked in at the sides of the coals. The ladies prepared tamales and enchiladas in abundance, and a constant supply of tortillas was patted. Brassy *mariachi* music led guests to the center of festivities where thirsts were quenched by *cerveza fuerte* — strong beer. The fandango was danced to a lusty guitar.

———————

The Heady Rose and Hardy Wine:
Mission San Juan Bautista

On March 2nd, 1779, an American named Joel Roberts Poinsett was born on the eastern seaboard. At the conclusion of the Revolutionary War, Master Joel and his family moved to Europe where they lived until 1788. Upon their return to the U.S., young Poinsett enjoyed many advantages in his Charleston, South Carolina home. He studied law for a short

Opposite page:
Hand-crank
Organ

191

period, and then a variety of other subjects. But he settled on none of these and drifted from interest to interest.

During the War of 1812 Poinsett was again absent from the United States, but later returned to win a seat in the South Carolina legislature. Then, in 1821, he was elected a member of Congress. Between 1825 and 1829, he served as Minister to Mexico, where he was frequently embroiled in embarrassing controversies, often resulting from his openly anti-Catholic attitude. Since his diplomatic abilities were obviously less than adequate, he was at last officially recalled to the United States.

This "diplomat" is nonetheless credited with two accomplishments — the first being his success in establishing the Masonic Lodge in Mexico City, the second requiring further explanation.

Natives living in Mexico at the time were particularly fond of an indigenous flowering plant — the nochebuena — which grew profusely throughout the region. Upon his return from Mexico, Poinsett introduced the plant to the United States, where it was renamed *Poinsettia pulcherina* in his honor. Its tapering crimson bracts even today provide delight during the Christmas season, and it is known throughout the United States by the single word, "Poinsettia." But at Mission San Juan Bautista, the 15th mission founded, it remains "nochebuena" — the "Good Night" — in reference to Christmas Eve and the birth of Jesus.

Thus it often occurs that an accidental happening, an

offshoot from the "real purpose," has an impact far greater than could be imagined. Such is the case with the gnarled, strange-looking black sticks that Fr. Serra brought with him from Mexico. Most observers would have pronounced them quite dead, but actually they were living plants — *Criolla* vines — from which came the many thousand acres of "Mission" grapes that nourished California's communities. Low in acid and late-ripening, these purple grapes were so generous in their yield that they dominated the California wine industry until the middle of the 19th century.

Criolla
Vines

Throughout the missions, wine was used for meals and social occasions, for trading purposes, and, of course, for Communion — the sacred feast. Though all the communities experimented with grapes, San Gabriel proved the most successful in producing wine and brandy in great quantities. The admixture "angelica" — three parts grape juice to one part brandy — was also developed here. The central and southern missions all succeeded to some degree with the mission grape, thus demonstrating the suitability of California's soil and climate to viticulture.

The
Wine
Industry

Jean Louis Vignes of France and William Wolfskill of Kentucky soon introduced new cuttings to the area. Vignes imported several varieties of Europe's *vitis vinifera*, and very quickly became the major independent producer of wine and table grapes in California. He also provided wines for the rapidly increasing number of ships visiting her harbors.

Even in its pioneering days the California wine industry

piqued the interests of people from a broad range of nations. Winemakers Charles Krug and the Wente family were of German origin, Sutter was from Switzerland, and Wilson of Los Angeles came from Ireland. Gustave Niebaum, who established *Inglenook*, hailed from Finland, while Drummond of Sonoma came from England. Perhaps the most influential of these early men was Agoston Haraszthy of Hungary. Colonel Haraszthy experimented throughout California, starting in San Diego, then moving to San Mateo and finally achieving his greatest success and reputation in Sonoma. The founder of *Buena Vista*, Haraszthy produced superb wines and contributed significantly to the development of the industry. In Northern California the Sauvignon Blanc cuttings from Bordeaux, France produced distinguished white wines, while the Zinfandel became the most popular red.

In addition to spawning the wine and cattle industries, other mission occupations gave rise to what are now successful secular enterprises. At Mission San Juan Bautista, the largely Mexican-American population sustains itself by fruit and vegetables growing, as well as other types of farming, a continuance of practices established during mission days.

San Juan Bautista, visually the most powerful of all the missions, came into being June 24th, 1797, in a fertile valley known to local natives as *Popeloutechoni*. Father Juan Crespi and Captain Pedro Fages had camped near here in 1772 (the valley is located about 35 miles northeast of Monterey and 90

• 21 SAN FRANCISCO DE SOLANO
• 20 SAN RAFAEL ARCANGEL
• 6 SAN FRANCISCO DE ASIS
• 14 SAN JOSE
• 8 SANTA CLARA
• 12 SANTA CRUZ
• 15 SAN JUAN BUATISTA
• 2 SAN CARLOS BORROMEO DE CARMELO
• 13 NUESTRA SENORA DE LA SOLEDAD
• 3 SAN ANTONIO DE PADUA
• 16 SAN MIGUEL ARCANGEL
• 5 SAN LUIS OBISPO DE TOLOSA
• 11 LA PURISIMA CONCEPCION
• 19 SANTA INES
• 10 SANTA BARBARA
• 9 SAN BUENAVENTURA
• 17 SAN FERNANDO REY DE ESPANA
• 4 SAN GABRIEL ARCANGEL
• 7 SAN JUAN CAPISTRANO
• 18a SAN ANTONIO DE PALA
• 18 SAN LUIS REY DE FRANCIA
• 1 SAN DIEGO DE ALCALA

miles south of San Francisco), but the area was not selected as a mission site until 1786. Nine years after that, Governor Diego Borica directed a task force of one corporal plus five soldiers to build the mission in honor of John the Baptist, and a year later, on June 24, 1797, Father Lasuen blessed the results of their labor. With the assistance of local natives, the man had by that time completed a granary, a residence for missionaries, a guardhouse, a barracks, and a temporary church overlooking the valley. Padres Jose Martiarena and Pedro Martinez then fell to work on a more permanent chapel, eventually completing a structure forty-two by seventeen feet. Yet the astonishing success of the new community demanded an even larger church, and hundreds of natives soon began this task — one that would require fifteen years to complete.

Converts laid the cornerstone on June 13th, 1803. The events of this day and the names of the personalities involved were committed to paper, placed in a small vessel, and inserted into the cornerstone to await some future generation.

The new church was constructed from local sandstone and adobe bricks weighing fifty pounds each and measuring thirty by sixteen by four inches. For the floor, natives formed *ladiellos* — kiln dried bricks measuring twelve by eight by two inches. Alders, poplars and willows were then cut for supports.

With its three spacious aisles, the structure at San Juan Bautista became the widest mission church. In 1809 the

195

community placed a carved statue of St. John the Baptist on one of two altars, and by 1818 the reredos and a third altar — the main one — were completed. As a result of the cinnabar used to color the mortar, the walls of the church remain rich and strikingly warm.

Difficulties arose when a Mexican artist named Chavez was selected to embellish the church interior. Although Father Arroyo — the priest assigned to the community — consulted at length with the painter, the two could not agree on a suitable fee. When Chavez played "hard to get," Arroyo commissioned one Filipe Santiago to do the work in return for just regular meals and a place to sleep. A sailor and self-taught draftsman, Santiago was among the region's first American settlers — in his hometown of Boston he was known as Thomas Doak. Santiago, or Doak, worked with a team of native artists at San Juan Bautista. Their bold, colorful and unlabored designs met with full approval from the community.

Additional statues were then added to the reredos. While the figure of John the Baptist remains the most conspicuous, visitors are also drawn to a likeness of St. Pascal Baylon at the uppermost center position. San Antonio occupies the upper left niche and St. Isadore commands the upper right. The lower left holds St. Francis, and the lower right, St. Dominic. Each figure is set against a scarlet backdrop.

December 12th is a particularly important feast day at San

Juan Bautista. Before dawn of that day community members

conduct a candlelight service in which a statue of "Our Lady" is carried in procession about town. The procession is followed by a day of feasting, celebration and great joy, echoing an event that began over 400 years ago.

On December 9, 1531, a native named Juan Diego stood on a hill outside of Mexico City. Suddenly there appeared before him a glowing image of the Holy Virgin — La Purisima Concepcion. Though she wore the familiar crown and did identify herself, Our Lady's appearance was not unlike that of an ordinary native woman. She instructed Juan to go to Bishop Zumarraga and tell him to build a church on the hill where they stood. Frightened and confused, Juan carried the message to the bishop as ordered, only to be dismissed as a fool. But the Lady of Guadalupe persisted, appearing on the second night, and the third, each time demanding from Juan a report on the progress of her church.

It was a very frustrated Juan Diego who returned to the office of the bishop on the fourth day. He could only assent when Zumarraga declared that he needed some evidence — perhaps a sign. Using the illness of a relative as an excuse, Juan tried to avoid another confrontation on the hill, but the Virgin came down to intercept him. When he asked her most reluctantly for a sign she directed him to gather roses, which she placed on his cloak. She then neatly folded the garment and instructed him to keep it closed until he stood again before the Bishop. Juan reported immediately, and as Zumarraga watched he unfolded the cloak. The roses fell to

Our Lady
of
Guadalupe

197

the floor, and on the cloth was a life-size image of Our Lady, just as she had appeared to Juan.

Today this famous cloak, or *tilla*, is preserved at Guadalupe-Hidalgo. Apparently woven of maguey, it measures about three by six feet. In many of the missions there is also a popular reproduction of this image as painted by J. C. Padilla. Our Lady of Guadalupe wears a pink brocade robe, over-painted with gold, and a star-studded, dark blue cloak. Around her neck is a ribbon which holds a small cross, and on her head is the familiar crown. Her palms are pressed together, and she stands on a crescent supported by the shoulders of a cherub. Our lady radiates an aura — all about her are rays of gold.

During the throes of revolution and struggle for independence in Mexico, it was Our Lady of Guadalupe who provided the people with a sense of commonality and unity, thus a sense of nationalism. She became the patroness of Mexico, of the natives, and finally, of all of the Americas. The community at San Juan Bautista maintains an abiding respect for its cultural heritage, and the fullness of Our Lady's symbolic meaning to Mexico and Mexican-Americans is celebrated each December 12th as an expression of living faith.

Today, those who visit the mission may find in its museum a variety of musical devices, including a number of bells previously maintained by the community. Of particular interest is a wooden wheel from which radiate four hollow,

two-inch-square arms. Clappers attached to two of the arms rap loudly as the wheel is rotated. This device was used as the call to worship on those days of liturgy which excluded the use of bells.

During mission days the community also made use of a wonderful music box which has likewise been retired to the museum. The box is actually a five-foot-tall handcranked organ whose tones were once thought particularly gay. Among its selections were songs designed to soothe the soul and to inspire "foxy" dancing; the one most loved and requested by the natives was marked simply "Number 3." The machine is also inscribed with the name of the maker and year of completion: Benjamen Dodson, 22 Swan Street, London, England, 1735.

The church at San Juan Bautista was originally designed to accommodate a community of more than a thousand, and during the mission's highest point that enrollment was actually achieved. Between 1797 and 1835 the padres baptised 4,100 people, and in 1823 they recorded a native population of 1,248. But like the others, this mission, too, had its share of grief. As if compelled to the place, the church sits almost squarely over the San Andreas fault. During one two-week period the community experienced as many as half a dozen potent shocks per day, and damage to the buildings has been considerable.

With encouragement from the community Msgr. Amancio Rodriguez vigorously promoted the restoration of the old mission in the mid 1970's. Mr. B. M. Taylor applied his knowledge of adobe construction, and was guided in his restoration efforts by that same craftsman-historian who had been so important to the restoration project at La Purisima 40 years earlier — Harry Downie — a man who had filled those years acquiring knowledge and authority in mission restoration. Father Lawrence Farrell also contributed his expertise, and further contributed the wisdom of all Ireland. (The padres of Old San Juan continue to delight in the exercise of "blarney," and it is not uncommon for an unsuspecting tourist to overhear an annoyed priest announce that the mission sundial is running a full second slow!)

The original members of this Christian community are buried among tall olive trees in the church yard. The last of the natives, Dona Ascencion Solorzano, who died in 1930, is interred by the church wall. Father Tapis, who founded Mission Santa Ines during his term as Father-President, is buried in the sanctuary.

All about the town is evidence of its Spanish and Mexican heritage: the original baptismal font carved from local sandstone, the wonderful music box which rests in the museum. Now, only in the imagination can be heard the song that so delighted the natives — selection Number 3 — *The Siren's Waltz.*

Agony and Abundance:
Mission San Miguel Arcangel

The founding of Mission San Miguel took place on a cool morning in 1797. Father-President Lasuen and Father Buenaventura Sitjar came forward in all their ecclesiastical finery to perform the ceremony as several bells were suspended from the lowest branch of a spreading oak. Men, women, and children from the native community of *Vatica,*   203

21 SAN FRANCISCO DE SOLANO
20 SAN RAFAEL ARCANGEL
6 SAN FRANCISCO DE ASIS
14 SAN JOSE
8 SANTA CLARA
12 SANTA CRUZ
15 SAN JUAN BAUTISTA
2 SAN CARLOS BORROMEO DE CARMELO
13 NUESTRA SENORA DE LA SOLEDAD
3 SAN ANTONIO DE PADUA
16 SAN MIGUEL ARCANGEL
5 SAN LUIS OBISPO DE TOLOSA
11 LA PURISIMA CONCEPCION
19 SANTA INES
10 SANTA BARBARA
9 SAN BUENAVENTURA
17 SAN FERNANDO REY DE ESPANA
4 SAN GABRIEL ARCANGEL
7 SAN JUAN CAPISTRANO
18a SAN ANTONIO DE PALA
18 SAN LUIS REY DE FRANCIA
1 SAN DIEGO DE ALCALA

The
New
Community

located just north of present-day Paso Robles on the Salinas River, gathered around the event.

After the cross was planted, the Father-President sprinkled holy water over the entire area, and a statue of La Purisima was placed upon a rude altar beneath the decorated oak. Here, the community celebrated its first liturgy.

Once dedicated to God, the mission was placed under the protection of the arcangel St. Michael — the most glorious prince of the heavenly militia — and Padres Sitjar and Antonio de la Concepcion Horra (the latter new to California) were given charge of the facility. The bells sang as fifteen native children were baptized on this first day.

Exhausted after the difficult trip from San Juan Bautista, whose founding they had just taken part in, the expedition of ten priests and soldiers slept at peace among the natives. With time, the community constructed a church measuring thirty-four by twenty feet, as well as a large residence surrounded by a palisade of sticks and brush. Within a year the members had added dormitories and completed irrigation canals.

Early in the life of Mission San Miguel, the first of several unhappy events occurred: one evening after dinner, the residing priests were overcome by violent stomach pains. When Father Prijol arrived from Monterey to assist them, he too developed cramps, became dreadfully ill, and died. The padres soon began to suspect poison, and their theory was confirmed when they learned that three natives had been boasting in the village that they had indeed done this. A community meeting was held, and the guilty natives were flogged in the presence of their families, a serious humiliation and loss of honor for those involved.

Later, during August of 1806, just as the new community was becoming active in the various mission industries, a fire began in one of the shops. The flames spread quickly from building to building, destroying the manufacturing facilities, granaries and storage sheds. All materials, implements, and grain were lost; the church, too, was badly damaged. Because of the rapidly growing population, the community petitioned the Spanish government in Mexico for permission to build a new chapel. In anticipation of approval the members manufactured and stockpiled construction materials in large quantities. (In the process they became so expert in the manufacture of tiles that these became a major item of commerce; tiles were sold to settlers as well as to other missions.)

The
New
Church

Therefore, the community was quite prepared to proceed with the new church when permission was given in 1816, even though solid corbels and rafters would have to be hewn and transported fifty miles. The present structure stands forty feet high at the apex, and measures one hundred and forty-four feet in length by twenty-seven feet in width. Erected on stone foundations, the adobe walls are nearly six feet thick. The community also constructed a quadrangle of two hundred square feet. The essential arrangement reveals the church and a long wing on its left side fronted by a desert garden.

After the outer structure was completed, the mission padre, Fr. Martin, imposed upon an artist who had been his friend and neighbor in Catalonia, Spain — Esteban Munras — to design the interior. After the community agreed upon certain basic designs taken from a book in the library, Munras and a team of native artists rendered a most resplendant interior. The walls are painted in blue to represent pillars, while the decorative designs include leaves, flowers and a splendid arrangement of borders. At the center of the church interior, and on either side of it, is painted the illusion of a high balcony. In the sanctuary, floral designs provide a foil for statuary. The magnificently painted pulpit attached to the wall of the nave is entered via steep stairs, and across from it rests a large shell painted in pink and green to honor St. James. At the center of the reredos — a lofty frieze supported by pillars — is the "all-seeing eye of God" which radiated rays of white and gold. At a point above the altar rests a truimphant San Miguel, the mission's patron saint.

Beyond the rail in the sanctuary are two wonderful old chairs — one of velvet, the other of tapestry portraying a woven image of doves. The legend associated with this latter chair claims that any maiden who sits on it has the promise of San Miguel's priests that she shall find a husband within a year.

The floor of the church is constructed of kiln-fired brick laid in alternating rows of squares and rectangles. And, as

could be anticipated in a mission where tiles were so expertly produced, the roof of the entire facility is a great sea of burnt red.

The most successful year for agricultural production at the mission was 1810, when over eight thousand bushels of wheat, barley, corn, and beans were put into the granary. In 1814 the padres recorded their largest Christian population — 1,096 souls were at home in Mission San Miguel.

During warmer months, native families built rough, flat-roofed brush shelters as summer dwellings. These were supported on one side by the permanent winter house; the flat roofs were used to sun-dry fruit. Scattered about the home were domestic utensils: storage jars, mortars and pestles, a variety of baskets; and strings of beans and peppers were suspended from the walls. Near the front door of each shelter was a large earthen jar containing fresh water. To keep the contents cool and clean, pieces of cloth were placed over it. Stretched and drying animal skins were pegged to the ground or attached to the side of the house as part of the tanning process. To maintain the home fires, piles of wood and twigs were also kept close by.

In the midst of prosperity, Mission San Miguel was again struck by tragedy when Padre Juan Cabot decided to lead several expeditions east into a settlement of natives who called themselves the *Tulares*. On the first of these occasions the padre baptised twenty-five sick and aging natives, afterwards moving on to the rancheria of the *Sumtache*. The

Sumtache, not knowing the purpose of the visit but aware that the missionaries had just come from their enemies the Tulares, attacked Fr. Cabot's party, killing two horses and scattering supplies. The skirmish ceased after a soldier shot a native woman.

These outsiders — the priests and soldiers who had come to California from Spain and Mexico — were a very mixed and unlikely group. The soldiers were by and large young men (some were actually no more than boys), grudgingly serving a tour of military obligation. Lonely, homesick, and surrounded by what they considered a hostile environment, the soldiers maintained calendars in order to mark off each day that brought them closer to going home. Individuals of lower rank spent many long hours in backbreaking labor, and the punishment for even a minor offense was severe. Senior officers suffered similarly crude conditions: their cold and damp accommodations at the presidio were cause for despair. Regardless of rank, the soldiers commonly hated conditions in California.

The padres were truly of another order. They were a very well educated group, many of them (including Fr. Junipero Serra) having already completed careers as university professors. As if boarding a spaceship for a distant star, they submitted themselves to the long voyage from Spain to the new land, realizing that they would probably die en route, or in some strange place at the end of their journey. For most of them, it was at least certain they would never see their families again, nor touch those things familiar to their youth. These remarkable, grey-robed padres were completely convinced of the merits of their mission; they were resolute.

Still there were those who, in selecting this way of life, chose badly. It was a lonely and difficult life in many ways, and some were simply unable to cope with it. Among these was Father Antonio de la Concepcion Horra, a young man and one of the padres assigned to Mission San Miguel. Within a month of his arrival the padre became pensive, and in the isolation between earth and sky, flowering plants and chaparral, he spent long hours conjuring with demons. His behavior soon became erratic and finally violent. Indeed, he grew so abusive that those around him feared for their lives: he kept dueling pistols beneath his robe, and, among other eccentric acts, put members of the community to work collecting and executing ants by the thousands. Eventually, Fr. Sitjar described his colleague's conduct to the Father-President at Santa Barbara, and after an examination by two surgeons at Monterey, Fr. Horra was declared insane. He was then relieved of all responsibilities and escorted to the College of Santa Cruz, Queritaro.

Because of another unhappy event (much later in time, after secularization), eleven murder victims share a common grave just outside the sacristy of the church at San Miguel. In 1848, a man named William Reed and his family occupied apartments in the mission convento. After years of poverty, Reed achieved some success in the cattle business, and, being more than a little proud, soon began to boast openly of his wealth. When five sailors arrived at the mission in need of accommodations, Reed lavishly entertained them, bragging all the while about the money he had amassed. As the afternoon came to a close, the sailors — deserters from a ship harbored at Monterey — expressed their gratitude to the Reeds and took leave of the mission. Upon mounting their horses they immediately began scheming, pledging to return that night. Later, when the house was asleep, the sailors entered in search of the money, but finding nothing they awakened the residents with a demand to "deliver." At Reed's refusal the sailors shot them all, leaving a mound of bodies on the floor of the convento. A posse was quickly dispatched and the murderers were overtaken near the sea. One of the fugitives escaped into the water — only to drown — while another was shot. The remaining three surrendered and were promptly hanged. Reed, his family and servants were interred in a single grave.

The land holdings of Mission San Miguel were extensive, but the community made good use of them. In the mountainous region between the mission and the ocean, a rancho called *San Simeon* was constructed. Here native converts built a house, cultivated the land, and raised horses and cattle. Sheep were maintained south of the mission, and at Rancho de Santa Isabel a vineyard was planted. At San Antonio natives raised barley and at Paso de Robles they grew wheat. In each of these outlying regions adobe buildings were constructed for the storage of grain. Eventually, the pueblo of San Simeon became the center of the whaling industry, and up the road behind the town Senator George Hearst built a frame ranch house overlooking the bay. His son, William Randolph, used this location to store and exhibit the treasures he had collected from around the globe.

California's
Natural
Larder

One of the many natural gifts introduced to the padres at Mission San Miguel were the hot springs and sulphur mud baths at Paso Robles. The natives had long been aware of the curative value of these springs, and in time the priests also learned to make use of their properties. California's natural larder contained an abundance of many other things that were previously unknown to the Spaniards, including a diverse supply of nutriments. Just as the major food supply of the Great Plains — the bison — was held sacred by natives in that vast region, an equal significance was assigned to the

The
Acorn

tiny acorn in California. Since oak trees existed in broken patterns from Oregon's Umpqua divide to the Baja Peninsula, the small nut quite naturally became a staple of native diets.

Acorns have high concentrations of tannic acid, and they must be leached in order to become edible. This was done in a number of ways: sometimes the nuts were covered with sand on a bed of charcoals and doused with water at frequent intervals; sometimes the meats were simply buried in mud. Both methods are essentially filtering techniques. Acorns can be made sweet by boiling, but pounding them with a

mortar and pestle prior to leaching produces an instant food.

Every home contained special baskets designed to facilitate the leaching process, while on the beach, basins dug in the sand worked equally well. Natives commonly lined their basket or basin with soft bark, then added the nuts, and topped the mixture with a layer of leaves to keep the water that was poured over it from washing the meat away. A still more convenient method consisted of boiling acorn pulp in a basket or earthen pot.

Even in California's dryest, rockiest regions, the knowledgeable native could identify many sources of food as well as medications and narcotics. Saccharine found in the "screw bean" was eaten directly from the tree or fermented to make a beverage. A number of varieties of the *mesquite* plant produce beans, and in some area these were a major food supply. "Careless Weeds" were eaten as greens. With lengthy preparation *agaves*, of which century plants are a variety, offered a sweet food that could be stored for long periods of time. And though some people find them a bit sour, the "Spanish bayonet" — a type of *Yucca* — produced a nice fruit. *Chia*, made from a sage plant, was extremely popular as it could be taken as a beverage or prepared in the form of cakes. In some parts of California natives feasted on *pinon*, or pine nuts, and in other places they enjoyed the fruit of palm trees. "Indian figs" — prickly pears — were generally available, as were berries, seeds, and bulbs in an almost endless variety. Beside their small adobe homes near the missions, new Christians cultivated figs, peaches, tobacco and

213

large tuna cactus. They feasted on crayfish, turtles, snails, caterpillars, and grasshoppers, as well as rabbits, gophers, and lizards.

Though they hunted several types of game, natives were careful to avoid those animals with which great powers were associated. Included in this group were eagles, coyotes and grizzly bears. To facilitate the catch, hunters employed poisons and traps, along with bows and arrows and a variety of spears.

The new Christians throughout California eagerly contributed their bounty of natural resources to the liturgical feasts. The preparation of food for others constituted a very special grace, and the calendar observed during mission days provided frequent opportunities for such activity. The most favored celebrations included *Corpus Christi Day*, the feast day of Our Lady of Guadalupe, the *Posadas* of the Christmas season, and *Judas Day*, during which members of the community flogged an effigy of the betrayer. On these occasions Christians filled the night sky with fireworks, and feasted as if there would be no tomorrow.

Community
Feasts

———————————

Opposite page:
Mission Oven

Coyote was walking down the road one day, feeling very lonely, when he met a Lady Tick. 'You are very darling,' he said to the Lady Tick. 'Will you marry me?' 'Yes darling,' said the Lady Tick, 'But I don't think I can travel as fast as you.' 'That is no problem darling,' said Coyote. 'Just jump and ride on my shoulder.'

"So the Lady Tick jumped upon Coyote's shoulder and they went on down the road. After a while it occurred to Coyote that his love might not have eaten recently. He asked her thoughtfully, 'Excuse me darling, are you hungry?' And the Lady Tick answered, 'It is very thoughtful of you to ask darling, but I just ate.' Coyote looked around and indeed her body was larger. They went on down the road for a while and it occurred to Coyote that his love might not have had a drink recently. He asked her thoughtfully, 'Excuse me darling, are you thirsty?' And the Lady Tick answered, 'It is very thoughtful of you to ask darling, but I just drank.' Coyote looked around and indeed her body was larger.

"They went on down the road for a while and they met a Lonely Deer. 'You are very darling,' said the Lonely Deer, 'Will you marry me?' 'Yes darling,' said Coyote, 'But I don't think that I can travel as fast as you.' 'That is no problem darling,' said the Lonely Deer, 'Just jump up and ride on my shoulder.' And that is the end of this story."

THE PLAINSONG

As the Christian tradition moves through time and space, little habits develop within the various communities which on occasion become customs, and even conventions, of the Church. Assuming that they are not held inviolable, thus restricting the development of new expression, these habits surround the tradition with beauty. They also contribute to an appreciation of "existence" or "being" in a meaningful way, and through them members of the various communities may learn something of the nature of the tradition in which they stand.

In California there were songs, gestures, events, objects, and images that properly fit this category. While they were not central to the tradition, and are not to be confused with the tradition, they cast a style and created a *richness that is always associated with the Roman Catholic Church.*

Of these habits, or devices, few were more compelling than the *Plainsong* — a musical vehicle which elevated and underpinned the "word" in the Franciscan missions. The term "plainsong" refers to a type of vocal music formalized by the Papal choir during the time of Gregory (circa 540-604) and subsequently adapted to all aspects of the Roman rite. Though it is an unmeasured musical form, meaning it exhibits no regular pulse, the Plainsong produced a concordance of euphonious sounds that highlighted the psalms and scriptures in various mission celebrations such as Mass or the daily choir services. On such occasions, it contributed significantly to the creation of a joyous emotional climate in California's Christian communities.

While the Plainsong typifies devices that influence the conduct of community members, the "Companionship of the Saints" was also a conventional part of mission reality. The lives of these individuals exerted a powerful influence on human conduct; and as communities formulated their response to external pressures, models provided by such personalities as St. Francis and St. Clare were constantly employed.

During religious training new Christians were instructed to refer to the saints when experiencing grief from any quarter. To prepare the way for this "companionship," the padres familiarized converts with each saint's life, and a specific positive human quality it exemplified. In time the natives became familiar with a great number of saintly personalities —there was a saint associated with every day of the year.

Specifically, natives were instructed that through meditation they could project their condition or dilemma out in front of them and to consider it from several angles. The saints were like so many pieces of colored glass held up between the individual and the problem: they cast it in a new light. In this way Christians regarded their own condition through the eyes of people who experienced life in its fullness, through the eyes of individuals who really "lived." It was via the gift of imagination that the saints came to intercede.

Some converts made use of several models, while others had a favorite saint, or relied on the one in whose custody their own mission was placed. The padres encouraged individuals to emphasize the *methodology*, or *process* that each saint employed — to consider the saint's commitment to, and intensity of, *being.* Yet mission history is shot through with tales of individuals who, being of a literal mind, sought to emulate their models in full detail. If, for example, a certain saint had traveled to Rome as part of his strategy in overcoming a problem, the convert felt that he, too, should make the trip. One may as well suspend judgment on these matters since evidence suggests California's converts routinely employed unlikely means with some considerable success.

In addition to the Plainsong and the companionship of the saints, mission communities further incorporated a number of visual images or icons. For example, each facility displayed

the fourteen "Stations of the Cross" in either three dimen-
sional carving, "bulto," or flat illusionistic painting,
"retablo." According to the various stages of Christ's passion,
they illustrate, at the First Station: Jesus is Condemned;
Second Station: Jesus Bears His Cross; Third Station: Jesus
Falls the First Time; Fourth Station: Jesus Meets His Mother;
Fifth Station: Jesus is Relieved by Simon of Cyrene; Sixth
Station: Jesus Meets Veronica; Seventh Station: Jesus Meets
the Women of Jerusalem; Ninth Station: Jesus Falls the Third
Time; Tenth Station: Jesus is Deprived of Clothing; Eleventh
Station: Jesus is Nailed to the Cross; Twelfth Station: Jesus
Dies on the Cross; Thirteenth Station: The Descent from the
Cross; Fourteenth Station: The Burial. In front of these images
(generally arranged along either side of the church) devotees
privately engaged in ritualized commemorative meditation.

Also conspicuous in the missions were the *milagros*, or
"little miracles." These are often small jewelry-like human
organs — hearts, arms, legs — cast from molds in gold or
silver. Upon recovering from afflictions of any part of the
body, members of the communities presented these analogous
tokens at a side-altar in thanksgiving.

A flood of other little silver medals were brought in from
Spain and Italy. By wearing this jewelry around the neck on
a chain, individuals placed themselves in the custody of their
favorite saints. Though the charms were not considered
"activated" until blessed by a priest, priests were not always

sympathetic to these requests — more than one padre was

truly vexed by the medals, feeling that the practices associated with them were very close to superstition.

In addition to making the sign of the cross upon entering and exiting the churches, Christians employed a variety of other gestures that contributed to mission experience. In deference to the Church as receptacle for the host (the sacred eucharist), members of the communities thought it impertinent not to *genuflect* or "bend the knee" when passing before the tabernacle. To provide for a gesture in which people of nearly all age groups could participate, the missions added tables of votive candles. These were sometimes lighted in conjunction with a vow, but more frequently the act was performed in gratitude or simply as a "good wish." Individuals who were so disposed might light a candle for their friends, their loved ones, or for themselves.

Another popular gesture was the "Saying of the Rosary." Conducted with the aid of a beaded string, this little act of piety consisted of a tight, repetitive utterance beginning with the *Ave Marias* and ending with a *Gloria*. While reciting, devotees were urged to meditate on the Christian mysteries.

Together the gestures, objects, images, and music, which is to say the "art" of the California missions, to a large degree *consituted* rather than embellished life in the communities. While no single habit was of essential significance to the tradition, tensions created by the interaction of them all generated a resonance and gave rise to meaning. Together they were a source of cohesiveness and social order.

Gestures
in
Mission
Life

The Art
of the
Missions

"Coyote was walking down the road one day. He could smell the moist earth; he knew that the World was new. Everything was dark because fire had not been invented, nor the sun, nor the moon nor the stars.

"He came upon a group of people who were singing and dancing. Coyote loved to dance, so he joined in. Together they danced and danced and danced. Coyote finally became worn out. He wished that the dancers would stop, but he didn't want anyone to know that he was the only one who had grown tired, so he kept dancing. Finally his head became very light. It floated up and away.

"He found himself in a place where Snake sat warming himself by a fire. Coyote asked if he could join Snake to rest for awhile. Snake was very polite, he invited Coyote to share his food and his fire.

"After a while Coyote told Snake that his friends the dancers would like some of that fire, and he asked Snake if he could take some back with him. Snake said that Coyote was more than welcome to some of the fire if he had

something to trade.

"Coyote searched his pockets, but found nothing. Then he remembered a story Snake might like. Snake said that Coyote's story would be fine, so Coyote sang the story to him. When Coyote was done Snake remembered the story and Coyote forgot it.

"Coyote woke up and it was daylight. He could hear the dancers, still singing. He looked at them and they were not dancers at all. Coyote was in a field; it was tall grass that was swaying and singing in the wind. Coyote walked on down the road, he was in the Valley of the Moon.

"Soon Coyote came upon a most beautiful woman. She had white hair and she wore a long dress made of white bird feathers. Coyote was so pleased to be with her that he began to show off and play the fool.

"The beautiful woman told Coyote that he should be more respectful or he would disturb Snake. Coyote very boastfully pulled up a large tree and began swinging it back and forth like a club. He told the beautiful woman that if she would tell him where to find Snake he would kill him. The beautiful woman smiled at Coyote and told him that he was too late. While Coyote had slept, Snake had eaten the land; they were now in Snake's belly. And that is the end of this story."

Our Lady and Her Consort:
Mission San Fernando Rey de Espana

Governor de Neve held a roster of the names of eleven families in one hand, while at his side hung a leather pouch containing the land contracts each had signed. This group, gathered together to found a pueblo, exhibited an interesting ethnic variety, its membership a blend of black, brown, and white. Among those standing on the banks of the Rio de

Opposite page:
Mateo, Marcus,
Lucas, Juan

231

Portiuncula were *Jose Navarro*, a forty-two year old man of mixed ancestry, his wife and three children, and fifty-year-old Spanish-born *Jose de Larra*, with his native wife and their three children. *Bastillo Rosas*, a sixty-eight-year-old native brought his wife of mixed ancestry and six children. A thirty-eight-year-old black man, *Antonio Mesa*, his wife and their two children, had come in from San Gabriel, as had native *Jose Vanegas* and his wife and child. A nineteen-year-old native named *Alejandro Rosas* and his wife arrived without children. There was *Pablo Rodriguez*, with his native wife and child, accompanied by their friends of mixed ancestry, *Mr. and Mrs. Manuel Camero*. Other members included *Luis Quintero* — a fifty-five-year-old black man, his wife and their five children; and twenty-two-year-old *Jose Moreno* and his wife, also of mixed ancestry. A thirty-year-old Spaniard named *Felix Villavicencio*, his native wife and child, completed the list. These forty-four people were the founders of the City of Los Angeles.

The story behind the name, "Los Angeles," is long and historically involved. To make the tale brief, the river along which Governor Neve and the settlers founded their pueblo was named in honor of St. Francis. Specifically, the river's name, "Portiuncula," refers to a chapel outside the Italian town of Assisi, the *Cappella della Portiuncula*, once used by St. Francis for asylum. That chapel also went by the name of *Maria degli Angeli* (Our Lady of Angels). Thus, "Los Angeles" derived from a combination of the two names for Francis's place, of asylum: "Nuestra Senora la Reina de los Angeles de Portiuncula."

Three such civil pueblos had been authorized by 1781, the others being San Jose de Guadalupe and Branciforte, both previously discussed. The individual specifically charged with recruiting settlers for the town of Los Angeles was Captain Fernando Rivera y Moncada. Traveling through the Mexican provinces of Sinaloa and Sonoma, Rivera managed to contract seven settlers and forty-five soldiers (the latter to be assigned to the presidio at Santa Barbara). But by the time he was prepared to move north, all the civilian settlers had faded. Disillusioned, Rivera finally left Sonora with thirty soldiers and their families.

At the Colorado River the party was met by an escort from Mission San Gabriel. Placing his charges under the protection of these guides, the captain and his men rested on the eastern banks of the Colorado. However, as the group slept a band of hostile natives slit the throats of the entire detachment: the "Yuma Massacre."

It was a later group of settlers, the forty-four people described above, who arrived at Mission San Gabriel on August 18, 1781 — San Gabriel being southeast of the projected site and the last stop on their journey to it. There, preparations were made for the final leg of the trip, the founding of this pueblo being sufficiently important that the governor would attend. On September 4th the party reached the site of Los Angeles to establish their new town. Beneath the Spanish flag, soldiers and natives participated in the founding of this civil pueblo. Then, the signed contracts secure in his pouch, Governor de Neve called the names of each family and made allotments of land. The house sites faced a plaza shaped like a diamond whose four points looked outward in the cardinal directions.

The local natives — members of nearby "Yang-na" rancheria — were largely indifferent to the day-long laborings of the settlers. The new residents, needing temporary dwellings until adobe homes could be built, set posts in the earth, tied cross beams, and made thatched roofs with brush and mud. Other responsibilities included cultivating gardens, constructing a dam and irrigation canals, and diverting fresh springs for drinking water. The settlers were pleased with the cooperative spirit at work; if a person was observed struggling with a log, for example, neighbors rushed to his assistance. Spirits soared as individuals, many of whom had never before worked a full day, threw themselves into the tasks at hand. But unfortunately, this euphoric condition was short-lived. Petty little annoyances piled up to break the spirit of community.

The first transgression occurred when Mr. Mesa failed to return a tool he had borrowed from Bastillo Rosas. Then, Luis Quintero broke another settler's adze and made no offer to replace it. While the same Quintero struggled to pile supplies by himself, Jose Moreno sat idly by and watched, even though Quintero had just given Moreno three hours of work for which the former received no expression of gratitude.

Then, a native boy presented Mrs. Jose Vanegas with a large string of fresh fish which she let spoil, even though it would have been equally convenient to have given them to Mrs. de Lara. Antonio Mesa noted that some of his storage grain had disappeared. While he could not prove a theft, Mesa remembered seeing Manuel Camero loitering about his shed. The Vanegas' boy had a fight with one of the Quintero children, a dispute that ended with the two families no longer speaking to each other.

Before six months had passed the community determined that the de Laras, the Mesas, and the Quinteros were not pulling their weight. After a secret vote the three families were expelled from the pueblo and the population of Los Angeles fell to sixteen. Jose Navarro and his family were also ordered away soon afterward, and in 1785, Jose Francisco Sinova joined the community as a replacement.

Conditions somewhat solidified, and the pueblo of Los Angeles developed rapidly. Twelve houses grew up around the plaza and twenty more dotted the country-side, all of adobe construction with thatched roofs protected by mud and by asphaltum discovered in the La Brea district. One of the settlers — Juan Jose Dominguez — received a generous land grant which became noted for its lovely hills and glorious view, and to which the new proprietor assigned his own name; he called another of his ranchos San Pedro. The community built a town hall, a jail, a granary, barracks for a few soldiers and, in time, a church.

For several years the residents of Los Angeles traveled to Mission San Gabriel for liturgy, though the distance and inconvenience of such trips eventually caused members to press for a church of their own. In 1784 a new chapel was dedicated to *Our Lady, Queen of the Angels*, and the small town that continued to develop around the plaza became known by the same name.

Twenty-three miles north of the Los Angeles pueblo, in an area now known as the San Fernando Valley, a mission honoring the Spanish King Fernando III was dedicated on September 8th, 1797. San Fernando Rey de Espana was the seventeenth mission to be founded.

21 SAN FRANCISCO DE SOLANO
20 SAN RAFAEL ARCANGEL
6 SAN FRANCISCO DE ASIS
14 SAN JOSE
8 SANTA CLARA
12 SANTA CRUZ
15 SAN JUAN BAUTISTA
2 SAN CARLOS BORROMEO DE CARMELO
13 NUESTRA SENORA DE LA SOLEDAD
3 SAN ANTONIO DE PADUA
16 SAN MIGUEL ARCANGEL
5 SAN LUIS OBISPO DE TOLOSA
11 LA PURISIMA CONCEPCION
19 SANTA INES
10 SANTA BARBARA
9 SAN BUENAVENTURA
17 SAN FERNANDO REY DE ESPANA
4 SAN GABRIEL ARCANGEL
7 SAN JUAN CAPISTRANO
18a SAN ANTONIO DE PALA
18 SAN LUIS REY DE FRANCIA
1 SAN DIEGO DE ALCALA

The
New
Community

As Fr. President Lasuen celebrated the dedication and first Mass, a detachment of soldiers from Santa Barbara and a large group of natives — those who had named the area *Achois Comihavit* — looked on attentively. The alcade (mayor) of the Los Angeles pueblo, Francisco Reyes, had been maintaining cattle here, and Spaniards knew the area as Encino Ranch. With the establishment of San Fernando Rey, however, missionaries were able to challenge Reyes' claim to the land. The padres soon made their home in the ranch house! Thus, San Fernando Rey reversed the usual pattern — rather than townsmen encroaching on mission lands, in this case it was the mission which took over lands claimed by pueblo members.

The church at Mission San Fernando Rey de Espana was consecrated in 1806. Guests from Santa Barbara and La

Purisima were entertained by a group of natives demonstrating their mastery of European musical instruments, the Spanish language, and Latin chants. Nonetheless, the occasion was clouded by the major topic of the day — political alliance.

With domestic problems occupying the energy of government officials in Mexico City, the remote California missions had come to be of little significance. As interest waned, so did financial support. In the meantime, the rapidly increasing population of California was thus forced to confront a question of loyalty: must they remain subjects of the King of Spain, or should they shift their allegiance to the tumultuous government in Mexico.

But Mission San Fernando Rey also had practical matters to resolve. They considered the supply of natural resources available in their environment and determined that the cattle business would provide the greatest opportunity for financial success. In fact, their passion for the industry caused them to be a bit cavalier, for in addition to its own grazing land the mission co-opted that of its rancher neighbors. On one occasion a very angry Pio Pico ordered the Christians to keep their sheep off his ranch at Simi, and at each suggestion that another secular rancho be established in the area, the mission community directed heated arguments and a flood of letters to the authorities at Santa Barbara.

By 1818 Mission San Fernando Rey de Espana was the home of more than a thousand converts. The gardens were

237

splendid, and in addition to grain the community grew olives and dates and picked grapes from 32,000 vines. The hide and tallow commerce was also successful.

These mission industries — the trades — were Father-President Lasuen's passion; during his tenure the missions achieved their greatest financial success. Prosperity was enjoyed by everyone associated with the facilities, even those who only spent a night in the community as guests. Convinced that natives needed a knowledge of the industries to build an economic base, the Father-President brought large numbers of tradesmen from Mexico to instruct the converts. Fortunately, Governor Diego de Borica also enthusiastically supported this notion, and it was he, in fact, who encouraged experimentation in agricultural products and techniques.

Borica was the most liberal of the Spanish governors. A military man and very able administrator, he authored progressive legislation on all fronts including the establishment of public education in the presidios and pueblos. Even though many of his ideas were not accepted, Borica remained generous in his proposals. He succeeded a string of officials that included Fages, Rivera, Neve, Romeau, and Arrillaga.

Upon the retirement of Gaspar de Portola, command finally passed to Pedro Fages. In general, Fages shall be remembered as an explorer, as it was he who led expeditions around San Francisco Bay. However, his relationship with the padres was less then intimate, and Father Serra once urged that he be removed from office.

Captain Fernando Rivera y Moncada replaced the unpopular Fages, and though his term was short, he is remembered as the leader of the second land party accompanying Portola's expedition. Actually, Rivera's leadership qualities were not well respected — he was eventually reassigned to a secondary position in Baja, and as previously recounted, was finally killed at the Colorado River.

Felipe de Neve proved a very ambitious successor. Trained as a military man, it was he who framed contracts for the establishment of pueblos and drafted the code of law and conduct enforced in both military and civil communities. When Neve received an appointment in Mexico, Fages served a second term as governor.

(It was during Fages' second term that Junipero Serra died. Fr. Francisco Palou succeeded Padre Serra as Father-President for a year, a position which had fallen to him because of seniority. But he had been trained as a historian, and he felt that his mission was to record faithfully the life of Junipero Serra. He therefore asked for reassignment, and was succeeded by Father Lasuen.)

Jose Antonio Romeau was appointed governor after Fages' second term. While Romeau was a competent man under ordinary circumstances, the serious illness he suffered during most of the term rendered him incapable of meeting the responsibilities of the office. It was during Romeau's tenure that Santa Cruz and Soledad were founded.

Following Romeau was Joaquin de Arrillaga, who, during   239 the second of two terms, founded Mission Santa Inez. It was also Arrillaga who died and was buried at Mission Soledad after the unsuccessful efforts of Fr. Ibanez to save him.

Diego de Borica served between Arrillaga's two terms. In addition to his vigorous support of the mission trades, Borica's cooperation with Father-President Lasuen made possible the founding of Missions San Jose (1797), San Juan Bautista (1797), San Miguel (1797), San Fernando Rey de Espana (1797), and San Luis Rey (1798). After Borica — and Arrillaga's second term — the appointment of Pablo Vincente Sola completed the list of Spanish governors.

During the turbulent years of Spanish rule, progress was made under each administration, but, in economic terms, the period which Father-President Lasuen and Governor Diego de Borica worked in concert was the most productive. It was during these years that the California missions achieved financial stability and a sense of fruition.

———————————

Opposite page:
Oversized, Illuminated
Book

ATÆ VIRG. ET [...]
n I. Vesp [...]
riósu [...]
e tri [...]

... sine macula,
nitatis lilium,
at quasi facula,
elo pereuntium.
i calcas sub pedibus,
misit ad fortia:
occurres hostibu[s]

Christi sufultus gratia.
Pugnat verbo, miraculi:
Missis per orbē fratribus:
Crebros adjūgēs sedulis
Fletus orationibus.
Trino Deo, et simplici,
Laus, honor, virt⁹, gloria:
Qui nos prece Dominici
Ducat ad cœli gaudia. Ā

IN I. NOCT. Ā.

Præco novus, et cælicus
missus in fine sæculi,
pauper fulsit Dominic⁹
forma prævisus catuli.

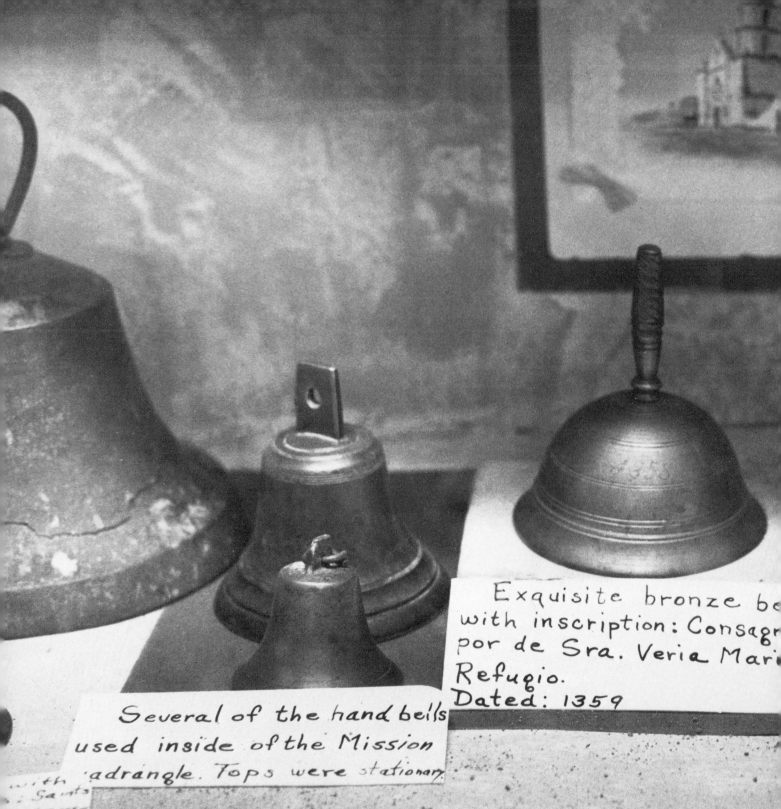

Several of the hand bells used inside of the Mission [qu]adrangle. Tops were stationary

with [...] Saints [...]

Exquisite bronze be[ll] with inscription: Consagr[ado] por de Sra. Veria Mari[a] Refugio. Dated: 1359

Father Peyri's Song:
Mission San Luis Rey de Francia

When Junipero Serra planted that first cross on the hill in San Diego, he could not have known that one of his future best lieutenants and the author of Mission San Luis Rey — Father Antonio Peyri — was just kicking the sides of a crib in Catalonia, Spain. In the chronicles of mission history, Fr. Peyri would be remembered as an extraordinary man among

243

extraordinary men. The facility at San Luis Rey is, in many ways, the long-cast shadow of this singular person.

Antonio Peyri's early years were not marked by events uncommon to other children. There is no record of his particular reasons for choosing the Franciscans, nor do we know why he specifically elected to do missionary work in "New Spain." We simply note that in 1796 he arrived at San Fernando College — the Franciscan headquarters in Mexico — to receive specialized training. And, on the 13th of June, 1798, we find him in the company of Fr. Lasuen at the site of the California mission honoring Saint Louis IX, King of France (1218-70). At that time Father Peyri was twenty-nine years old.

The location selected for Mission San Luis Rey overlooked a verdant valley less than five miles from the ocean, nearly forty miles north of San Diego. Here, the new community would enjoy almost continuous sun-filled days. In the company of Captain Grajera and his guard, as well as a few converts from San Juan Capistrano and a large number of local natives, Frs. Peyri and Santiago — the latter having also been assigned to the new mission — conducted the founding ceremony.

San Luis Rey has a more open and expansive quality than the other Franciscan communities. It was also the last mission founded by Father-President Lasuen and the last to be established in the 18th Century, closing the gap geographically between San Diego and San Juan Capistrano. Fifty-four

21 SAN FRANCISCO DE SOLANO
20 SAN RAFAEL ARCANGEL
6 SAN FRANCISCO DE ASIS
14 SAN JOSE
8 SANTA CLARA
12 SANTA CRUZ
15 SAN JUAN BAUTISTA
2 SAN CARLOS BORROMEO DE CARMELO
13 NUESTRA SENORA DE LA SOLEDAD
3 SAN ANTONIO DE PADUA
16 SAN MIGUEL ARCANGEL
5 SAN LUIS OBISPO DE TOLOSA
11 LA PURISIMA CONCEPCION
19 SANTA INES
10 SANTA BARBARA
9 SAN BUENAVENTURA
17 SAN FERNANDO REY DE ESPANA
4 SAN GABRIEL ARCANGEL
7 SAN JUAN CAPISTRANO
18a SAN ANTONIO DE PALA
18 SAN LUIS REY DE FRANCIA
1 SAN DIEGO DE ALCALA

children were baptized the first day, and seventy-seven more were joined within a week.

Members of the community spent their initial **days** manufacturing adobe bricks. Then, after trees had been cut and timbers fashioned, they delivered 175 beams to the mission site. Two years later, the 337 residents were tending gardens and maintaining 600 cattle and 1,600 sheep.

Father Peyri was of a democratic mind, and as more and more converts were embraced by the community, he supervised an election in which two natives, known as *Felix* and *Telmo*, were chosen to share the responsibility of alcalde (mayor), while *Mateo* and *Alejo* were selected to maintain order in the native community.

Following the padre's directions all mission structures were erected around a square measuring five hundred feet on each side. One by one, rooms were attached to each other along the convento, and by 1802 the chapel was complete and each building had been roofed with tiles.

During this period of rapid growth and prosperity, some disconcerting news electrified communities up and down the coast. At a time when international politics were already a major concern and nervous citizens expressed their loyalties quite cautiously, reports from the north revealed that a group of Russians had landed at Bodega Bay with the intent of establishing a community. The year was 1812.

(Earlier, in 1806, it was nothing but physical hunger that

guided the first Russian ever to make port at San Francisco Bay, handsome Prince Nikolai Rezanov. He had come from Sitka, Alaska, where Russian settlers were at the edge of starvation. In San Francisco he hoped to obtain supplies in sufficient quantity to preserve his colony, but authorities there were reluctant to aid potential enemies. However, by winning the hand of lovely *Concepcion Arguello*, daughter of the commandante, Rezanov was able to overcome these difficulties. After a mutual pledge of undying devotion, and Nicolai's promises to return and make Concepcion his bride, the Russians sailed a fully laden ship out of San Francisco harbor. Concepcion waited for many years, finally joining a convent, but Prince Rezanov never returned to California.)

The 1812 expedition, led by Ivan Kuskov, was designed to establish a permanent settlement and supply post at Bodega Bay. With the aid of his comrades — fishermen, woodsmen, and soldiers — Kuskov built a well-protected fort on the natural bench one hundred feet above the surf. Then, behind a barrier of cannons and thick walls he erected a house as elegant as any north of Mexico City. Glass windows were installed and ornately carved hardwood furniture appointed the rooms; lush carpets covered the floors. It is not surprising that Californians were nervous — Ivan Kuskov was obviously here to stay.

Kuskov's men then constructed a wharf at the shoreline, granaries, work sheds, and a domed Orthodox chapel that included chimes. They built a bath house and cleared the beach for swimming, while Kuskov himself entertained with fine china and silver. A staff was assigned to cater to his every wish. Here, at what was initially called "Fort Russia," and subsequently "Fort Ross," the colony planted fields and gardens, again reflecting a desire to have permanent roots.

To assess the rather sensitive situation, the military governor (Arrillaga) sent an emissary to call at the fort. However, the messenger was able to relate only one happy note: though the fort was impregnable, the Russians were terrible farmers — food was in short supply.

When authorities in Mexico City learned of the foreign colony, they demanded that Kuskov leave the area immediately, as his settlement represented a violation of the treaty between Spain and Russia. Though Arrillaga himself carried the message, Kuskov simply ignored it; the Russians held every military advantage.

When Pablo Vincente Sola — the last of the Spanish governors — took office, he was shocked and angered to learn that California ranchers were supporting Fort Ross through trade. Farmers supplied the colony with food while the Russians offered valuable metal plows and other farm implements in exchange. Sola sent word that trade was to stop and the Russians were to vacate, but again the colonists paid no attention. Instead, they stepped up their industry by launching four new ships in the growing harbor and taking sea otter by the thousands if not millions. By 1840 the Russian colony had virtually wiped out the population of seals, sea lions, and otter along the entire north coast. Even seagulls were killed by the hundreds of thousands.

The ambition to maintain Fort Ross finally gave way as more and more American settlers moved into the area, making it clear to the Russians that while they could maintain their fort, they would not be able to expand. Moreover, the cost to the Russian Government became significant (the fort never did pay for itself). In 1824, the Russians gave up their claim to land in Oregon, and in 1842 they left California. All of the supplies, equipment, and weapons of Fort Ross were purchased by Johann Sutter, who used them to appoint *Sutter's Fort*, New Helvetia (Sacramento).

While the drama at Fort Ross was beginning to unfold, progress continued at Mission San Luis Rey. By 1811 the community had outgrown its church and was at work on a new one. Following the model provided by the Great Church of San Juan Capistrano, Father Peyri and the community also selected the ambitious cruciform style. An aerial view indicates that the configuration is like a crucifix — a long nave with a crossing transept in which side altars were constructed. Light enters the nave through a dome constructed at the intersection of the two segments. Just inside the church are two doors: the one at the left exits to a patio; the one at the right leads to the mortuary chapel — an octagonal room below a painted dome. In this chapel a statue of the Purisima rests on a recessed altar. Numerous paintings can also be seen in the octagon, as well as tables of votive candles, and at its

corners stand columns joined by brightly colored arches and rendered to look like marble. The walls of the mortuary are beautifully painted with repeating designs over a wainscot moulding. This small area was designed so that members of the community could maintain a vigil over their deceased loved ones. The altar itself is curved in a classic design — not unlike the foot of a large vase.

To their new church, the natives added a choir gallery in which two musicians were employed to tend the musical library. Here, an illuminated manuscript was conveniently placed on a revolving stand, accessible to singers who positioned themselves around it.

On either side of the nave are four large pilasters, splendidly painted with apparently random designs. At the front, on each side of the altar, are brackets which accommodate two of the five major saints. The other three have lofty positions on the reredos, but the crucified Christ in the center of the backdrop remains the most imposing figure. Numerous beams cross the gaily painted nave, and all surfaces are charged with color. It is a truly festive and memorable interior.

Situated on the crest of a hill, this church continues to enjoy a spectacular position, though it is now much reduced in size. But during mission days the rest of the compound rambled over many acres. In front of the chapel, community members constructed a fountain and a sweeping amphitheater composed of columns and arches. An open stairway followed the slope of the hill to a stream of fresh water surrounded by trees, flowers, and inviting paths. Here native women often chatted noisily as they sewed, washed clothes, or wove material. At other times, the area proved a delightful place to quietly sit in the sun.

At its high point, the mission occupied an area of about thirty square miles. There were broken fields of grain and gardens, and fruit trees growing both randomly and in neatly ordered rows. During the season that the trees were heavy with fruit, one native woman in particular (considered a terribly cunning and frightening figure) was assigned the duty of keeping children out of, and away from, the orchard. She enjoyed some success, since the tricks and devices she employed gave rise to fantastic horror stories circulated among the five to twelve-year-olds. As part of her strategy, she allowed each young person to speculate on the hellish tortures which would undoubtedly be their fate if caught in the orchard. Actually, Momma Vandalia never caught a soul in the quarter of a century that she watched over the gardens of San Luis Rey, and never really tried to. But the children, terrified because of the stories that she herself had propagated, attributed their escape only to the fact that she was large, and slow on her feet.

At one point, natives of San Luis Rey tended 27,500 head of cattle, an almost equal number of sheep, and 2,000 horses. There were also pigs, goats, ducks, chickens, geese, and family dogs to be fed. This was by far the largest of any mission community. By 1826, there were 3,869 converts making their homes here, and over 7,000 baptisms had been recorded. In almost every category, Mission San Luis Rey de Francia set records.

When choosing mission sites, the padres naturally favored locations where there were large populations of natives. But, of course, there were many native villages quite distant from any compound, and to provide for the people there, missionaries needed to establish little satellite facilities, or annex churches. At first the priests rode "circuit," visiting several rancherias and routinely conducting liturgy at each location. Then, as these new communities developed, each was permitted to construct a church of its own. It was not uncommon for a mission to support several such facilities, or *asistencias*.

A particularly successful asistencia was established at Pala, the site of one of six ranchos maintained by Mission San Luis Rey. Pala was located at the foot of the Palomar mountains less than twenty miles east of the facility.

Father Peyri dedicated the asistencia to St. Anthony of Pala — an early Franciscan missionary. After the dedication of the site in 1816, natives built a church 144 by 27 feet. The beams were simply trees from which the bark had been removed, and across these supports saplings were placed close enough together to hold the roof tiles. (Boards have subsequently replaced the saplings). The walls are rough, decorated with meaningful designs in earth colors, and the floor is of porous brick. This church exhibits a unique directness and vigor; being wholly without pretense, it is patiently disarming.

During its first years of existence, Mission Asistencia San Antonio de Pala was the home of over 1000 converts, and was assigned a permanent padre. Specialized buildings, including a school, were eventually erected, and gardens were planted.

Today, the asistencia continues to minister to the natives of Pala Reservation. The school is still in operation; the church and the museum, staffed by Native Americans, are quite correctly a source of considerable pride. And to everyone's delight, the community's unique, free-standing campanile remains intact. Following the design of a structure in Juarez, the natives built their bell tower completely separate from the church. Over a cobblestone base, a superstructure of cement and adobe is interrupted by two arched windows — one above the other — each containing a bell. The tower is surmounted by the familiar cross, next to which grows a fetching little cactus, high above any obvious source of nourishment.

While the Pala asistencia developed at a comparatively leisurely pace, San Luis Rey spent the turbulent middle years of the 19th century trying to adjust to the increasing number of demands from several essentially erratic Mexican governments. It was because of political difficulties that Father Peyri eventually realized he could no longer offer effective leadership to his community. He had fought with the

253

Mexican officials so often that everything he tried to do for the mission was met with hostility. Therefore, after considerable reflection the padre decided the interests of San Luis Rey would be best served if he removed himself from the mission altogether.

At sixty-three years of age Father Peyri arranged to leave the community that had so completely occupied his productive career. Believing there was no graceful way to part with his many friends, the padre secretly mounted a horse one night in January of 1832 while the community slept, and rode to a ship in the harbor at San Diego.

At dawn, with the discovery that their priest was absent, five hundred natives galloped across country in pursuit, but the ship was already clearing the harbor when they arrived. Standing on the afterdeck, Father Peyri saw his community for the last time. From horseback, the natives silently exchanged with their priest the sign of the cross.

With respect for his vow of poverty, Fr. Peyri delivered himself to the convent in Mexico with no worldly goods, and petitioned for whatever charity his Order might provide.

———————————

Opposite page:
  Pala's Freestanding
  Campanile With
  Cactus

A Matter of Judgment:
Mission Santa Ines

The people of the village of *Maljalapu* spent a summer in 1804 fraught with misfortune and complexity. The troubles began when three young men simultaneously presented themselves as leaders of the community, an unheard-of occurrence. Old and tested loyalties were fractured; nothing was secure; the community felt split.

Opposite page:
Prickly Pear
Cactus

257

Then, on September 15th, a momentous day for this village, a boy who had attempted to capture an eagle returned to the village empty-handed and nearly dead, blinded by cuts and gashes.

It was an ordinary practice for young men to capture eagles, and a particular, prescribed method was followed. First, a pit large enough to contain a person was dug; the eagle hunter then concealed himself in the hole which friends covered with branches. For bait, a large piece of meat was conspicuously placed over the hunter's head, and when a passing eagle dropped from the sky to take the food, the young man grabbed for its legs and pulled it into the hole. Then followed a life and death struggle in which the youth, if he was successful in avoiding the talons, strangled the bird in the prescribed, ritualistic manner. But on this day, September 15, 1804, in the hills beyond Maljalapu, the method failed and the eagle reigned victorious.

In late afternoon of that same day, news of approaching strangers quickly spread through the village. Two hours later, nine mounted soldiers appeared in the distance, followed by twenty-four natives and four grey-robed priests, each carrying a bundle of some kind. As they entered the village, two of the priests seemed at ease, while another appeared pleasant, but aloof, and the fourth nervously greeted everybody with a broad smile. A child observed that this latter gentleman waved his arms like a fat bug trapped on its back, a comparison thoroughly enjoyed by the community, and later explained to the embarrassed priest by an interpreter. While the padre acknowledged what was indeed a humorous remark, he still had trouble finding something with which to occupy his hands.

This group was welcomed by native women who appeared with chunks of meat and large quantities of irregularly shaped loaves of bread. These were passed among the guests who, following the custom of courtesy, first bit their food, and then cut it close to their teeth with sharp knives. After this most gracious feast, the natives listened intently as Father-President Estavan Tapis explained why the missionaries had come to their village.

At this spot, located thirty-five miles across the mountains from the Santa Barbara presidio, a mission was dedicated to God on September 17, 1804, and placed in the custody of the fourth-century martyr, Santa Ines. St. Agnes was a Roman girl who was executed at the age of thirteen. Despite bribery, threats, and finally the prospect of death, Agnes remained firmly obedient to her convictions. It is even reported that she went forward to be beheaded "more cheerfully than others go to their weddings." Her life continues to serve as a model of constancy.

Commandant Carrillo of the nearby Santa Barbara presidio witnessed the founding of Mission Santa Ines, while Fr. Tapis led the ceremony. Twenty-seven children were immediately baptized. The community built a church that was, if not elaborate, most certainly a joyous place for celebration. This

259

building served its members until the famous earthquake of 1812, when a corner of the structure fell. The granary was then emptied and used for services, but by 1817 a new and more imposing chapel was completed.

The largest membership in the community occurred in 1816 when 768 names appeared on the roles; by 1821 Santa Ines was also maintaining 12,368 large and small animals. The community developed a successful hide and tallow industry, as well as an impressive range of crops including corn, beans, wheat, and barley. The surplus from these industries was such that the presidio of Santa Barbara was provided with food and supplies valued at over $10,000.

While community progress was nearly continuous, an event transpired in 1795 that severely disrupted mission life and changed the role of Santa Ines. A directive drafted by King Carlos IV and distributed to all of the missions decreed that Spanish was to be the official language in California. To facilitate instruction in towns and religious communities, natives were henceforth forbidden to speak their own language.

The padres despaired over the directive. It was an outrageous order — destructive to the culture and impossible to implement. The priests had achieved some success with language instruction by tutoring individuals who were particularly gifted in music and wished to participate in the liturgy, but this had been a limited project. The resources for wholesale general education were simply not available.

A quick survey of the presidios indicated that illiteracy was also very high among soldiers. Even though military regulations prohibited men who could not read and write from advancing to the rank of sergeant, it was common to find less than ten percent who could meet this qualification.

In civil pueblos the level of literacy was equally discouraging, but in response to the King's directive a retired sergeant named Manuel Vargas took the first step toward improving this condition: in 1795, he opened a school in the San Jose granary. Each family was obliged to send their children, along with thirty-five cents per child to support the school. Other educational facilities followed. On February 25, 1796, a sailor opened a facility at Santa Barbara, though after he was called away to sea the project was abandoned. During the same year, a carpenter started a classroom at the San Francisco presidio and then was soon replaced by an artilleryman who received an incentive of $2.00 per month. Manuel Vargas moved to San Diego where he was paid $100.00 per year for operating a school attended by twenty-two pupils.

As they gained the necessary resources, each community hired a teacher and implemented the common academic schedule; no classes were held during the summer months when children were needed in the fields, and primary instructional emphasis was placed on Christian doctrine, followed by reading and writing (those who demonstrated these gifts were also taught to cipher).

The educational system in California thus began to grow, while in response to King Carlos' directive the languages of native California were systematically suppressed.

Mission Santa Ines was particularly successful in emphasizing education, at least partly due to its unique location. Since it was somewhat off the main trail, visitors were few, and in this isolation, academic study became a particularly respected activity. In 1843 a seminary — The College of Our Lady of Refuge — was opened here.

However, it would be erroneous to assume that the facility was continually peopled by bookish souls who spent their careers free of hostilities. Here, as at other missions, years of growth were punctuated by periods of pain, the most unfortunate incident occurring in 1824.

After 1821 Mexico, preoccupied with internal problems, no longer provided support for the California presidios. Soldiers, in need of supplies, turned to the missions (which were otherwise free of taxes). Initially, the detachments promised to pay for any supplies received, but the only payments made came in the form of unhonored drafts. Objections were raised by native members of mission communities, followed by a series of intimidating acts on the part of the military and a demand that the missions deliver all their surplus to the presidios. The situation erupted in February of 1824, when a soldier at Santa Ines flogged a native from La Purisima. The Christian natives rallied in the latter's support, arming themselves with bows and arrows and attacking the military guard, but their weapons were no match for army muskets and two of them were shot. Also during the melee, the structures of Mission Santa Ines caught fire.

As the blaze reached the church a truce was called. All hands — both military and native — worked together to put it out, then afterwards resumed the struggle! Sniping went on throughout the night, but with the arrival of a military detachment from Santa Barbara presidio the next morning, the natives fled to La Purisima.

The Seige
at
La Purisima

There they mounted cannons on the palisades and waited for the inevitable seige. For nearly a month they maintained control, but as news of these events was carried to the Governor, all available men were immediately dispatched to the fortification. Within two hours large cannons brought by the soldiers destroyed the mission walls — and the lives of sixteen natives. Charges were filed, and a quick trial at the presidio resulted in the execution of seven more converts. Long prison sentences were imposed on eighteen others.

The
Governor's
Judgment

The padres of both La Purisima and Santa Ines immediately rushed to the presidio, where they argued vigorously in behalf of the natives. But the government no longer had to take the priests as seriously as they had in the past, and the priests were less effective now in their role as spokesmen for the natives. While this tended to increase the bond between padres and natives, it did not help the particular persons involved in this case. The Governor judged that such punishments were necessary to avoid incidents in the future.

A Question of Pride:

Mission San Rafael Arcangel

In 1815 the padres of San Francisco de Asis acknowledged an alarming mortality rate at their mission. Many of the converts were anemic, while large numbers of others died from diseases such as measles brought by the Spaniards. Numerous respiratory diseases also developed, due at least in part to the dampness of the region; and the fact that converts

Opposite page:
Native Basket

265

were living in missions, rather than in accustomed ways, did not help.

Members of the community enlisted a variety of healers and curers, both Spanish and native, to bring an end to such epidemics. The practitioners produced several general-purpose elixirs: jimson weed — a plant not unlike belladonna — was applied to wounds; sacred bark was used for respiratory diseases and skin problems; and concoctions of several plants, though primarily tobacco, were taken internally or applied locally as prescribed by the healer.

A special group of native doctors relied exclusively on these techniques, supplemented by hot, salt water baths. Consulted only for minor complaints, such healers charged little for their services. Another group employed ceremonial procedures that included songs, dances, and the making of images. These physicians used no medications whatsoever, nor did they attend to symptoms, but concentrated instead on clearing the way for the body to heal itself.

The third and most expensive group of native doctors displayed their healing techniques during elaborate nighttime ceremonies. These practitioners exercised extraordinary powers — including the ability to kill from a distance, and a unique familiarity with the various uses of poisons. As a result, they were both respected and feared by natives and missionaries alike. Included in their procedures was the use of the "sucking stick" — a hollow tube which was pressed against the affected part of the body. The disease was sucked out through the stick by the healer, who then spit it into his hand for all to see.

The Spaniards relied partly on their knowledge of plants and the properties of blossoms and roots for medication. They also let blood and employed simple surgical procedures.

At Mission Dolores (San Francisco de Asis), the community explored every technique and concluded that the situation warranted construction of a sanitarium. The padres first conducted an experiment in which several sick natives were transported to a region of continuous sunshine across the bay. To their delight a general improvement was observed within days. Two hundred and thirty more converts were then removed to the warmth of *Nanaguani* — the native village on the opposite coast. Though Mission Dolores was short of priests at the time, Father Gil y Taboada, who had acquired some knowledge of medicine and the treatment of diseases, volunteered to head the new settlement. The project was approved by Father-President Payres, and on December 14, 1817, the missionaries planted the cross at Nanaguani and dedicated an asistencia hospital under the protection of St. Raphael — the arcangel and messenger who announces the healing of God.

Natives welcomed the new Christian settlers and aided their cause. Twenty-six children were baptized the first day and large numbers of adults made themselves available for instruction.

Though the padres had envisioned future construction of a

The Mission
Is
Founded

267

small rancho and chapel, San Raphael essentially was to be a medical facility. The first project undertaken was a single building eighty-seven by forty-two feet — a hospital, in fact — containing partitions to divide the space as necessary. As needs increased, however, this structure was eventually enlarged and a surrounding convento was added. The next buildings to be erected were storerooms and a kitchen. Finally a church was built, the facade of which was simple yet elegant, as it contained a star window copied from the one at Carmelo. Near the front entrance, bells were suspended in an open framework.

Since each building faced out from the side of a hill, San Rafael enjoyed the long rays of the sun. All about the grounds were trees of every kind, and the sounds of birds filled the air. The warmth, cleanliness and medical attention provided by this community quickly came to be prized, and the northern missions eventually transferred all their sick and wounded to its facility. By 1820 the community was caring for 590 persons. Moreover, the mission became successful at gardening, at raising cattle, and at trades. Not only were they able to become self-supporting and independent, they were even able to deliver a surplus of goods to the presidio at San Francisco. Though it was never intended that San Rafael function as anything other than an asistencia, it was awarded full mission status in 1823 in recognition of its achievements. By 1828 more than a thousand natives were making their homes here.

The pleasant little hospital was squarely situated in a region famous for a number of distinguished Native American warriors. There was *Marin*, a heroic native warrior who, in response to the injustices committed upon his people, harassed the military for years. Marin County is named in his honor. Then there was *Quentin*, another native who struggled to live free from the constraints of civilization. His name is now associated with a point on the bay. Finally, there was *Pomponio*, whose motives were perhaps more selfish, since the target of his raids included native villages as well. A remarkable tactician, he committed numerous robberies and murders, evading capture for some time. But on the 6th of February, 1824, the militia found him hiding in Canyada de Novato and immediately transported him to Monterey, where he was tried and shot.

In the meantime, the relationship between Mexico and Spain, which had been deteriorating for years, gave way to Mexican cries of revolution. All of California's missions were deeply affected by months, and then years, of political turmoil. Finally, in 1822, Governor Sola convened a caucus at Monterey. Calling the presidio commanders and mission padres around him, Sola announced that Col. Augustin Iturbide of the Royal Army, aided by revolutionaires in Mexico City, had successfully instituted himself as commander of the new and independent nation, Mexico.

The padres quickly swore their allegiance to the Mexican government, nonetheless hoping that through negotiations with

269

the King of Spain, Mexico's colonies, including California, would remain under Spanish rule. However, it was not long before a ship arrived in the harbor of Monterey flying the red, white, and green flag of Mexico, and Augustin Fernandes de San Vincente disembarked to announce that the days of Spanish authority in California were over. The high romance of Dons and Princes, of royal appointments and intrigues, was to be no more. A *nacional* government, non-imperialist, democratic, was to take its place.

Political
Unrest

A galloping egalitarianism soon swept through California, accompanied, inevitably, by erratic political changes.

Iturbide had no sooner established himself as Augustin I, Emperor of Mexico, than he fell from favor. A succession of leaders — none of whom gained the strength of popular support — then came to power in the new republic, and California was pulled first to the left and then to the right as rapid changes swept the unstable Mexican capital.

In 1822 Luis Antonio Arguello was appointed in Mexico City as Acting Governor of California. The word *imperial* was struck from public buildings, and the word *nacional* was inserted; the title *Don* immediately lost fashion. Still, grassroots support for the Mexican regime was not strong, and prompted by their own progress at the local level, the Californians themselves became "nationalistic."

Luis Antonio
Arguello

The province quickly lost all financial support from Mexico. In response, Arguello established a *junta* comprised of representatives from the presidios and pueblos, then formed a committee to devise methods of filling the provincial coffers. Turning its attention directly to the missions, the committee recommended a tax levy on California. The padres protested, arguing that the land belonged to native members of Christian communities, and was therefore not subject to taxation. Such rebuttals were not well received, however. The Mexican administrators, knowing that the missions controlled the richest lands and the most vigorous industries, concluded that the uncooperative padres deserved a reprimand, though they were careful not to make it a public one. Others suggested the missions be removed altogether from the custody of the church.

In 1825, after only 3 years of service, Arguello retired as Governor of California. Nonetheless, significant economic gains had been made in the province during his tenure. His regime had done much to inspire trade with merchants from the eastern seaboard, and under his auspices a number of American companies were established in California. The shipping industry, too, had been encouraged, and there was a flourishing trade in hide and tallow, well described in Richard Henry Dana's *Two Years Before the Mast.* Though this was an era dominated by political and social upheavals, a sense of romance and adventure also pervaded. Scotch whiskey was brought to California in large quantities, and social life grew more prominent. It was also during these years that Concepcion Arguello, the governor's lovely sister, maintained her vigil in unrequited love for the Russian Prince Rezanov.

Jose
Echeandia

Arguello himself was succeeded by a tall, thin hypochondriac — Jose Echeandia — who conducted the affairs of state limp-wristed and with a hankie at his nose. Governor Echeandia, a unique amalgam of frailness and pomposity, headquartered himself in Old Town San Diego, whose economic base was now secure enough that citizens had ample leisure for social considerations. Echeandia was quite generous with his favors about town, singling out the beautiful Senorita Carrillo for particular attention. Citizens twittered as the Senorita alternated between gentle Echeandia and robust Henry Delano Fitch, a dashing young American ship-captain. In response to this new and polite society, the city fathers resolved that, henceforth, horse dung would be routinely removed from public thoroughfares. Culture was on the rise in San Diego.

Despite the govenor's social finesse, however, political maneuvers caused him great difficulty. The Mexican regime provided no treasury for him to operate the local government, and soldiers assigned to the presidios went several years without being paid. With time the populace revolted, and a kind of "paper revolution" was conducted: declarations and pronouncements were nailed to walls, doors and trees. But the Mexican government persisted in its indifference to the protests, further alienating the citizenry through practices such as exiling criminals in California. When seventy-five thieves and murderers were delivered to Santa Barbara, local citizens in turn deposited them out on the Channel Islands. This was

Criminals
Imported
to
California

but a temporary solution, as the criminals soon cut trees, fashioned rafts, and rowed back to Carpenteria.

Still Mexico continued to send its problems by the shipload. Fifty more criminals arrived, then eighty, and then another twenty-five. The Californians took to distributing them equally among the communities where they could be under local supervision. Many of these desperate men joined the military, and others even obtained public office.

Echeandia, either apathetic or perhaps simply weak, was ineffective in mediating the difficulties between California and Mexico. It was he who capitulated to factions demanding that California's missions be transferred into civil pueblos; and it was he who finally announced officially the intention to secularize all mission facilities. But his successor, Colonel Manuel Victoria, though strongly opposed to secularization, received no warmer reception in California. In fact, Victoria's early conduct alienated people in great numbers. Perhaps trying to be helpful, this stern military man declared war on rampant crime in California. However, he invoked the death penalty for even minor offenses, and citizens began to shudder at his name. Victoria, racked with insecurity, discouraged public meetings and the flow of information by establishing layers of command, protecting himself by an impenetrable network. Those who spoke against him were executed or banished, and mission padres lost the privilege of representing natives charged with crimes.

Victoria ignored countless letters and petitions from citizens,

Manuel
Victoria

273

while the *diputacion* — an elected legislative body — attempted unsuccessfully to confront him with matters of state. After refusing to meet with them for a period of time, Victoria declared that the representatives had been illegally elected and were to convene no more.

Such oppressive techniques rallied many otherwise disparate interests. Distinguished California families — the Bandinis, the Picos, the Carrillos, and the Alvarados — dissociated themselves from the governor altogether, publicly renouncing their allegiance to him. They finally demanded his resignation, insisting that military and civil leadership be held in two separate offices. Following their guidance, a band of rebels committed themselves to armed combat. They overtook San Diego's presidio, and then marched to Los Angeles, where they gained control and support for their revolution.

Following these events, a formidable army of insurgents was quickly mounted — over two hundred citizens marched up the Camino Real with the intent of throwing Victoria out of office. North of Los Angeles they met the governor on his way down from Monterey. Victoria urged the rebel soldiers to either put down their arms or join him, but a charismatic and daring Jose Maria Avila answered the ultimatum by riding out alone, drawing his sword, and singly charging Victoria and his lieutenant Pacheco. Avila galloped past, missing both men, but then turned, drew his pistol and shot lieutenant Pacheco in the heart. Avila himself was killed during the battle that followed; Victoria was wounded and forced to withdraw. As a result, the governor relinquished his office, which was then temporarily returned to the weak Echeandia.

The *diputacion*, which had been disbanded, re-assembled and met in Los Angeles. They appointed a successor, announcing in January of 1832 the selection of Pio Pico. Echeandia exploded, refusing to relinquish his post to a Californian, but by December the protest was of little consequence: Jose Figueroa had arrived from Mexico to assume the governorship. It was now apparent, however, that any outside leadership would raise serious objections. Californians, on the threshold of a new order, prepared to take charge of their own destiny.

Pio Pico

MISSION
SAN FRANCISCO SOLANO

At the Edge of the End:

Mission San Francisco de Solano

The profile of those who now called themselves Californians changed during the 1820's when California's first large wave of immigrants arrived. Though many came from Europe, most of the new settlers had traveled from the American eastern seaboards where, as businessmen of all kinds, they were abandoning their old careers in search of new lives. These

Opposite page:
Votive Candles

277

were often individuals who, in their former occupations, had gained reputations for sharp or exploitative business practices. But here in California, they at least pretended after new habits, new life-styles and acute social consciences. For reasons good or bad, they made genuine commitments to their new homes. And California, in turn, was good to them. Talented entrepreneurs quickly gained fortunes by serving as importers and exporters, as merchants in the hide and tallow industries, as suppliers and outfitters, and as tight-fisted money-lenders. Having acquired new wealth and new virtue it was now possible for them to marry into prominent families; and with their new wives and social status they participated in mission community activities.

Even in the most secular of environments, such as the larger cities, mission ties with the local community at large were many and complex. When the churches were not being used for group functions, they were available for private meditation, and men, women, and children made frequent visits to reflect upon their blessings. The ladies, accustomed to covering their heads upon entering a chapel, carried or were provided with *mantillas* — head scarves — often of fine Spanish lace. These intricately detailed veils tended to obscure the faces of the visitors, thus lending an ambiance of modesty and discretion to such occasions.

Members also made use of their churches for the purpose of *reconciling* their lives. In the privacy of the confessional, Christians shared with their padre any incidents or habits that corrupted an otherwise positive and productive existence. Then, in meditation, members reflected upon ways in which they might turn their lives to new directions, or at least select other points of focus.

In addition to these functions the missions also served as centers for dialogue. The padres, who in the main exhibited a high regard for the life of the mind, created many opportunities for the discussion of books and significant ideas. And, as controversial notions of social reform gained support throughout California, Christian communities often became the scene of heated and volatile debates. Liberal ideas were asserted here, and there was talk of a new order, of revolution, and finally of independence.

Church as Information Center

By 1822 a shift in the profile was discernible in those missions around which large cities had developed. The natives, generally unhappy with urbanization, had gone inland or to more remote mission facilities, so that membership in urban mission communities was now largely made up of the new merchant class.

Such were the conditions at San Francisco's Mission Dolores when the very young Fr. Jose Altimira was assigned to that facility. Upon leaving his native Spain, Fr. Altimara had eagerly anticipated the challenges and hardships that undoubtedly lay before him in California's wilderness. However, he found a different kind of hardship at Mission Dolores, where he was given only minor responsibilities in a community staffed by priests now well advanced in years.

Father Jose Altimira

The anxious padre sensed that the facility had lost its purpose, that it was no longer responsive to the natives. And feeling smothered by ancient men who had long since become complacent and lethargic, he was open and biting in his criticisms. Dismissed as petulant, the young padre quickly lost favor.

Altimira then took his cause to Governor Arguello, who, for motives of his own, was far more responsive. The padre argued that mission Dolores at San Francisco, where the native population was very small, should be closed, and its supplies and equipment used in establishing a new mission to the north among a larger group of natives. The governor agreed, calculating that such a mission might also arrest the threat of additional Russian development there. The 1823 Territorial Assembly approved the plan, further stipulating that the hospital mission, San Rafael, should also be closed to contribute its functions to a new mission.

It was a gleeful Father Altimira who traveled north with nineteen soldiers from the San Francisco presidio in late June of 1823. After days of searching, the party discovered a particularly favored spot in the "Valley of the Moon." In order to distinguish it from the old mission, soon to be razed, Fr. Altimira named his new facility "New San Francisco." With the assistance of local natives, the padre began construction of a church; and before the end of August a granary was completed, ditches were dug, and corrals were built.

280   However, on the 31st of that month, Fr. Altimira was

recalled to the city of "Old San Francisco" to answer for his impetuous conduct. It appears that the young priest had functioned in a completely peremptory fashion, having cleared none of his project with Franciscan officials, who were only now hearing rumors of a new mission. In no uncertain terms, Fr. Superior Payera ordered Altimira to stop construction on the church and to return to his duties at Mission Dolores. But Payera died before the order was enforced, and the problem fell to Fr. Senan, the new Superior, who also died shortly thereafter. Thus, all of Fr. Altimira's elderly detractors removed themselves as obstacles to his plan. The next administrator, Perfect Sarria, did not wish to stop progress on the new mission, but was unwilling to close Dolores or San Rafael, and so all three facilities were permitted to continue.

Fr. Altimira returned to the Valley of the Moon, where he directed construction of a wooden house for himself, and where, on Passion Sunday, April 4, 1824, he dedicated the church. However, since the notion of an "Old" or "New" San Francisco remained somewhat sensitive, the padre did not insist; he shifted the name slightly, and called the new community *San Francisco de Solano* in honor of a missionary who had served in Peru. The diversion was quite successful: for many years the new mission was known simply as *San Solano*.

Thus, fifty-four years after Fr. Serra planted the first cross in San Diego, the twenty-first and final mission was officially founded. But, because the facility built to honor St. Francis of

Asis was being called *Dolores*, and this final mission had been named after another Francis, the padres were again without a facility to recall the name of their famous founder and guide.

The
Mission
Facility

By the end of 1825 Mission San Francisco de Solano enjoyed a complete multipurpose adobe building measuring 120 feet in length by 30 feet in width. And, though the structure was only seven feet high, it contained a covered corridor and the familiar tiled roof. The community also worked on two additional buildings, which they completed except for the roofing, but winter rains melted the adobe walls, reducing them to irregular mounds of mud.

The city (Sonoma) which grew up around the mission remained exclusively a native community for several years. Of the 690 persons residing there, the majority were transfers from San Jose, San Rafael and Mission Dolores. The Russians of Ft. Ross also proved to be good neighbors, presenting a number of gifts to the mission and attending the dedication of the church.

Johann
Sutter

Later, when the Russians decided to leave California, Captain Johann Sutter of Sutter's Fort paused here during his expedition to buy the guns and equipment they were leaving behind.

Sutter was an interesting and a generous man. After gold was discovered on his property, about seventy-five miles east of Sonoma, he entertained hundreds of guests there — at his "Fort of Great Friendship." Numerous squatters also settled on his land, and between the encroachers and the guests, Sutter lost or gave away his land and almost all of his wealth.

Finally he and his family were forced to leave, and he spent the remainder of his years trying to recover some of his former holdings and claims.

After Sutter's departure, a substantial city developed around his fort. Though the citizens struggled unsuccessfully at first over a name for their community, a compromise was eventually reached. It was decided to name the town after a nearby river, one the Spaniards had christened to honor the Holy Sacrament — *Sacramento.*

Meanwhile, a treaty ratified in 1819 placed Oregon under the control of the American government, setting California's northern border some several hundred miles above San Francisco de Solano. During the period of Mexican rule, Governor Figueroa sent Mariano Guadalupe Vallejo north to explore this territory and identify several sites for possible development as presidios. Vallejo established an estate for his own use in the Valley of the Moon, though he was also responsible for the establishment of two secular communities in the area: *Petaluma* to the west and *Santa Rosa* to the north. *Pe-talu-ma* is a native exclamation, "Oh! fair land," while Santa Rosa honors "Rose of Peru." Legend tells us that she was a native girl of great beauty who, in her youth, felt troubled by her own *vanity.* She purposely destroyed her lovely complexion by applying hot peppers and quick lime to her face, and when ordered to wear a wreath of beautiful

Petaluma

Santa Rosa

283

roses, donned them as a crown of thorns. Pope Clement X was asked to canonize her, however he refused, retorting sarcastically: *"Indis y Santa! Asis como llueven rosas!"* ("An Indian woman a saint! This may happen when it rains roses!") And indeed, legend has it that a shower of roses immediately began to fall on the Vatican, ceasing only when the pope agreed to Rose's sainthood. Santa Rosa may still be found in the California missions; she is distinguished by her thorny crown, while in her arms the Christ Child rests on a bouquet of roses in full bloom.

The town named after her, Santa Rosa, represents one of the more successful efforts to establish a secular community in northern California. By contrast, there were some distinct failures. In 1834, years after the Vallejo expedition, a man named Jose Maria Padres attempted a commercial venture in this area, leading over 200 settlers from Mexico into the Valley of the Moon. This project had financial backing, and its constituency was made up of professional people, including teachers, lawyers, doctors, surveyors, artists, and engineers. Also among this group were a number of administrators with designs on public office. But despite the bevy of talent in this group, and the fact that it had at least initial governmental support, the project was doomed to failure. Californians closed ranks against the Mexican "outsiders," and without an economic base, they were eventually forced to turn to the charity of Mission San Francisco de Solano. Later, many were absorbed into the towns in the Valley of the Moon. The founder of the colony, Jose Padres, who had envisioned great wealth coming from his project, railed against Governor Figueroa for his lack of support, but was rewarded for his efforts by being exiled to San Blas.

Governor Figueroa was himself an outsider — a Mexican — and with sentiments running so high against non-Calfornians, it would seem difficult, if not impossible, for him to provide effective leadership. But he was an extremely bright and educated man, and possessed a unique ability to mitigate upheavals and adjust to the perplexing issues to which he had fallen heir. The most difficult and emotionally charged of the problems he confronted was *secularization*. The missions, theoretically, had now outlived their usefulness. They had served their purpose in securing the California territory for Spain and Mexico, and secular communities had grown up around them, as envisioned. The original plan had called for the missions to be established for only a ten year period, after which time they were to be secularized. The Mexican government argued that the time for this had come. The fact that the missions had large holdings of some of the best lands was also a strong, if unspoken, argument.

Secularization

Governor Figueroa was convinced that this was a serious mistake, that these Christian communities, particularly the native members of these communities, would suffer. Nonetheless, officials in Mexico demanded that he press forward.

In August of 1833 came the final decree that all mission

facilities in Baja and Alta California were to be converted into civil pueblos under secular control. The land was to be parceled out to individual members of the communities, to work, sell, or otherwise dispose of as they saw fit, while the natives were to be "emancipated."

———————————————

A Long Stillness:

The Period of Secularization

The Tree at the Center of the World trembled. Although Governor Figueroa attempted to effect the change as efficiently as possible, and with concern for the lives of those involved, the period of secularization took its own inevitable course through history, some 65 years after the first mission had been founded in San Diego. The missions were not secularized all at once, but in general the following pattern applied: mission resources were divided into two equal parts, and one half of the property and animals were given to secular officials to be sold. The proceeds were then used for city improvement, construction of schools, and adminstrative salaries. The remaining share of land and livestock was apportioned to members of the communities by the padres. Upon receiving their collective wealth, some of the natives immediately drifted away to start life anew further inland; others remained near the missions, the only homes they had ever known.

One by one these living, growing communities fell before the singularity and one-dimensionality of secularization. All twenty-one were abandoned; all twenty-one were finally, and quite inexorably, dead.

In November of 1833, Figueroa secularized Mission San Juan Capistrano, calling it a "provisional pueblo." There is no record of the disposition of foodstuffs and inventory, but we know the lands were divided among 140 persons, of which 100 were natives. The church and the pastor's house remained in the custody of the pueblo, while all other structures were sold at auction. After 1844 no priest was in residence.

San Luis Rey was secularized at the end of 1833, after which the facility, functioning as the barracks for a Mormon battalion, quickly began to deteriorate. The palisade in front of the church washed away and nearly all of the tiles were

stolen. The uncovered walls of the buildings then eroded, so that only the arches along the corridor remained in tact.

In December of 1834 the library at Mission San Rafael was sold for $108.00. The padres distributed 1291 sheep and 439 horses among over 300 native families, while General Vallejo conscripted the community's best horses for "military defense." The buildings were eventually deserted, and though Fremont used the church as his headquarters for a short period, no maintenance was provided — the entire facility fell and was washed away. For a number of years the site was occupied by a wood frame building constructed as an armory.

In 1841 small amounts of gold were discovered at Mission San Fernando Rey, after which hundreds of amateur prospectors descended upon the mission to dig up the entire area. It is interesting to note that for purposes of sifting the ore, gold seekers used shallow native baskets called "bateas." These proved to have such an efficient shape that they were later duplicated in metal. The native name soon gave way and "gold pans" were manufactured in large numbers throughout the west. Souvenir hunters took what the gold seekers missed at San Fernando Rey, and the only building maintained was the long house, which was pressed into service as a pig barn.

By 1844, nothing remained of the community at Mission San Miguel. The natives had dispersed, and the convento was first rented, then sold; small businesses, shops and apartments were later established in the wing. At one point the Howe Sewing Machine Company had a retail outlet here, and for a number of years Mission San Miguel served as a liquor store, a smoke shop, and a bar.

In 1844 a smallpox epidemic killed the majority of the population that had remained on the grounds at La Purisima. It was in a state of ruin when it was sold in 1845, fetching a price of $1,110.

Ten years after secularization, 30 natives still made their homes at San Carlos Borromeo de Carmelo, living among its decaying buildings. But by 1852 the roof had collapsed and the buildings were totally abandoned. The chapel was used by cattle that grazed on Carmel's gentle slopes.

Father Doroteo Ambris served San Antonio de Padua as curate for thirty years, doing his best to stay the destruction of time and vandals. However, as there was no one to replace him when he died, the buildings gradually deteriorated; the walls melted to a fraction of their former size.

In 1840, horse thieves descended upon Mission San Luis Obispo. Twelve hundred of the animals were driven off by enough bandits to discourage all but token efforts to stop them. By 1844 the entire community was scattered, and the next year the mission sold for $510.

When secularization was first instituted in San Gabriel, Mexican officials ordered that the 5,000 head of cattle owned by the community be slaughtered, rendered into hides and tallow, and the proceeds divided. Government employees performed the labor, returning only 1,000 hides to the

community. In 1845 the mission was declared valueless,

except for extensive vineyards that were rapidly deteriorating. Two hundred and fifty natives remained at their homes on the site, but having no means of support, they were eventually forced to drift away.

Mission San Diego de Alcala was secularized in 1834. By 1836, citizens of the local pueblo were loudly protesting the presence of natives who remained on the old property, claiming objectionable conduct on their part. A few civilian groups even made raids on the mission, during which several natives were killed. In 1837 a scheme of retribution was organized with the help of native servants in the homes of wealthy San Diego families. At an appointed hour, these servants were to unlatch the doors of their employers' homes and permit the entrance of armed conspirators. However, the plan failed when one of the servants alerted his employer; all of the conspirators were then arrested and shot. By 1845 there were less than 100 natives in the region of the old mission.

At San Juan Bautista the name of the pueblo community was changed, for a period, to San Juan de Castro. A substantial community of Europeans, Mexicans and Americans developed, though for several years the town suffered occasional attacks by local natives. In retaliation, citizens conducted a series of armed expeditions in which the attackers and their villages were completely destroyed.

In 1843 the mission grounds at Santa Ines were rented for $550; the next year the lands sold for $1,700. When the mission stores and other inventory were conscripted in 1845, the resident padre was pressured to sign a document confirming this action as an approved "loan." He refused, and soldiers stripped the entire facility. After 1850 even the church was abandoned.

In 1845 Mission San Francisco de Solano was declared to be of no value. However, 35 years later the facility and surrounding lands were purchased for $3,000, and the church building was thereafter used for hay and wine storage.

At the close of the same year, Mission San Buenaventura was leased for $1,600 per year. The renters, Narcisco Botello and Jose Arnez, greatly increased their investment within days by selling the community's flourishing crops and abundant resources.

At San Jose and Santa Clara, mission lands were sold to provide revenue for the pueblos, and when Fr. Sarria died at Mission Soledad, that community, too, died out. By 1850 there still remained a few random huts around the mission, but no new generations were to emerge from them.

Thus, one by one, the Franciscan missions of California gradually perished. Spiritual matters were taken into custody by the ghosts who remained.

———————————

Rebirth and Restoration:

Sir Harry Downie, Architect

In June of 1891 a lone dove hunter wandered about behind San Diego's old mission. Suddenly, a small, yet sturdy sapling growing out of one of the ruined adobe walls caught his attention. A careful examination revealed that when the old mission was first built, seeds had been embedded in an adobe brick, and throughout all the years of mission life they had

Opposite page:
El Camino Real
Marker

297

remainded dry, protected, and dormant. Then, when the roof fell and the top of the wall was exposed, rain water had seeped into the hardened mud, bringing the seeds to new life. Now, a young tree grew at this lofty position.

Finding this phenomenon interesting, the hunter discussed it at dinner that evening, and it was decided to have a picnic at the site the following weekend. On that occasion the family broke bread among friends and discussed the innate beauty of ruined San Diego de Alcala. The idea of trying to salvage the mission church appealed to them, though they noted the difficulties and high costs involved. While they were talking, one of the men, as a gesture toward clearing the debris, picked up and tossed aside a piece of broken tile.

In October of 1891, the *San Diego Sun* featured an article describing the efforts of a devoted group of citizens to restore Mission San Diego de Alcala. Luckily, enough of the building remained intact to make such a project possible. Further, the original bells of Junipero Serra's church had been located in various places: two in the Old Town Chapel, one in the military barracks, and several others scattered elsewhere about the grounds. Six bells were found in all, and a follow-up article in the *Sun* reported on the community's progress.

At Mission San Luis Rey, the church was rededicated on May 12, 1893. Honored at that time were three old native women who had actually attended the original dedication in 1802. Also present were the bishop and vicar-general of the Franciscan Order, as this facility was now the home of a community of Franciscans studying for missionary service.

On July 3rd, 1882, four hundred people gathered at Mission San Carlos Borromeo de Carmelo for an occasion pivotal in terms of restoration activities. In the sanctuary, a heavy stone slab was removed, exposing the redwood coffins of Fathers Crespi, Lopez, Lasuen, and Junipero Serra. While the coffins themselves were not disturbed, the lids were raised and the contents examined. Later, after the floor was replaced, several baptisms were celebrated at this location; Carmelo began to flourish anew.

At abandoned San Antonio de Padua several concerned residents had removed the appointments of the mission for safekeeping. When restoration was undertaken in 1904, the objects were returned to their respective places and a new roof was added.

At San Juan Capistrano, the local parish priest, Father John O'Sullivan, took charge of the restoration project. Numerous photographs of this small, deeply committed padre still remain today. In several of these, the volunteer laity are pictured engaged in backbreaking labor — removing and rebuilding — as the stormy Irish priest reigns over them.

In 1851 four Jesuit priests, four lay professors and twenty-six students opened the doors of a college at Santa Clara, bringing that old Christian community to a new academic existence. At Santa Barbara, too, a school and training ground for Franciscans was established, as well as a center for Franciscan resources.

As each mission became responsive to the integrity of its individual voice, community after community blossomed anew. The man frequently responsible for this rebirth was Mr. Harry Downie of Carmel.

Sir
Harry
Downie
K.S.G.

As a child Harry Downie had been profoundly impressed by the missions. It was significant to him that he walked where others had walked, that the past was continuous and unfolding. Though membership in his own Christian community provided him with a sense of *who* he was and *where* he stood, it was the mission event that told him *when*, that gave Mr. Downie his indisputable position in an ongoing history.

Born in Eureka Valley on the 120th anniversary of Fr. Junipero Serra's death at Carmelo, Harry Downie was destined to hold a place in the rich history of California. The entire Downie family, in fact, held a historical consciousness. His father was a native son, and served as a member of the El Dorado Chapter of the Native Sons of the Golden West. His mother, too, had been born in California, while Harry's

Early
Years

great uncle had founded *Downieville* in the Mother Lode country.

Harry himself spent his early years besieging Fr. John Sullivan, the pastor at the Mission Dolores parish, with endless questions about the old missions. Clearly impressed by the enthusiasm of this inquisitive young man, the priest assigned him various repair jobs around the Dolores facility.

And, recognizing that the youth himself had a calling — a

"mission" — Sullivan arranged for Harry to serve an apprenticeship in Hunt's Cabinet Shop on Sutter Street in San Francisco.

Harry's mentor — Hunt — was a fine cabinet maker educated in Germany, whose work was much in demand in San Francisco. From him, the young Downie learned methods of working with hardwoods to produce finely crafted furniture. He assisted constructing the altar and rail of Mission Dolores' splendid new Basilica. Then, upon becoming a Master Craftsman, Harry was called to Hearst Castle where he rendered further assignments in hardwoods. Numerous commissions followed, among them those at the Flood, Crocker and Stanley Dollar estates.

Harry maintained alliance with another old friend and mission enthusiast, Fr. Lawrence Farrell, who had served Mission Dolores as sexton and Mission San Carlos Borromeo as curator and guide in 1931. In the fall of that year Fr. Farrell presented Harry to Father Philip Scher (later to become Bishop Scher), who employed the young craftsman as curator. From that time forward Harry Downie's total energies and devotions were directed toward the California Missions.

In his work Harry enjoyed the encouragement and support of his lovely bride, Mabel McEldowney, who later presented him with two daughters.

To carry out his special task, Mr. Downie studied every detail of mission structure and building technique. He then cut, nailed, sawed, excavated, plastered, poured and tiled

301

throughout the missions. He moulded adobe bricks, carved saints and painted reredos.

Requests for his assistance were made by the communities at San Juan Bautista, San Antonio, Soledad and San Luis Obispo, while the State of California urged his participation at La Purisima and Sonoma. He was consulted at numerous facilities including Los Angeles and San Diego, and has worked closely with, and enjoyed the respect of, Fr. Maynard Geiger, O.F.M., the Franciscan authority on California mission history. Mr. Downie supervised the construction of the museum at Mission Dolores, and personally carved the Purisima at San Francisco de Solano. His name has become synonymous with the restoration of mission communities.

These renewed communities have not failed to recognize Harry Downie's unique contributions. He has been honored by the Knighthood of the Papal Knights of St. Gregory, and by the Knighthoods of Isabel la Catolica of Spain and of Castillo Belvar (Palma de Mallorca). A special plaque honors his name in the Carmelo chapel. Friends celebrate August 28, the feast day of Junipero Serra *and* the birthday of Sir Harry Downie.

As time passes, Mr. Downie's most significant contribution to the missions may prove to be his endless research into mission history. He laboriously collected and preserved documents and photographs from each facility, finally accumulating a library of each. Within this body of knowledge lies the agenda of Christian communities striving to come to terms with their historical role.

Today, there is a temptation to point to obvious stylistic origins in the California Missions: this is native, that is Spanish, this is Italian, Roman or Mexican, and to stop there. But, of course, it is not so simple. The Franciscan Missions are particular *and* peculiar to California. The materials themselves are indigenous. The wall-paintings and the crafts executed by native converts continue to provide powerful archetypal images — no mere gestures in behalf of Christianity. Native values and native expression inform and are infused in the multiplicity of design and construction. It could not really be otherwise. In California the Christian message was written by the native hand. And both traditions, that of Native America and that of Roman Catholic Spain, remain in evidence, though both have taken on new dimensions because of the interface.

The story of the missions is a tale of fact and fancy from which one might learn of good and evil, of generosity and grace. It is also the story of Native America, and of men like Fr. Serra and Harry Downie — Christians who brought a feast to their communities.

The emblem of this celebration of being, the tree that rose in San Diego, lives on — mature and generous, vital and loving. The Franciscan missions of California are once again living Christian communities. Standing in traditional authority, they retain the power of an unfinished past.

Acknowledgment

It is a great pleasure to recall the names of even a few of the very many generous contributors to this account of the mission event. For their support and encouragement beyond apparent limit, I am first of all indebted to my immediate family: Beverly, Bric, Bret and baby sister Nancy. And I should like to mention my "extended family": Joseph Epes Brown, James W. Flanagan, Robert W. Funk and Ray L. Hart, who for more than a decade have remained stimulating colleagues, patient teachers, and joyful friends.

Also among those who have contributed in a quintessential way, I must cite Mr. John Woodenlegs of Lame Deer, Montana. And I am, of course, deeply indebted to the numerous priests, Native Americans and the members of the various California missions who so kindly shared their stories about their communities, and thus provided the bulk of this material. Of the numerous individuals associated with these communities it is a particular pleasure to mention Father Lawrence Farrell of Monterey, California who, in addition to providing the information about his old friend, Harry Downie, shared with me a profusion of tales about these Christian communities. The late Father Maynard Geiger, O.F.M., also a friend of many years, was a very positive factor during the early stages of this work.

Ms. Sara Miller, my Graduate Research Assistant, yet already a "pro," contributed in countless ways, as did Sally La Trielle and Sue Seymour who typed, and retyped, the manuscript.

I am indebted to Robert Weissinger and his associate, San Diego's eminent portrait photographer, Paul Oxley, as well as Bruce Steinbrecher and his crew at Missoula's "Darkroom," for the extended use of their enlarging facilities. My thanks also to Helen Melnis of the University Graphics Department who generously permitted me to use her shop.

Included in the *Bibliography and Additional Readings* are the numerous publishers who unselfishly gave permission to adapt material from their publications. And the native basket illustrations in this book are here through the generosity of the San Diego Museum of Man, the staff of which made it possible for me to photograph their collection.

In addition to the individuals in each of the California missions who were helpful as I struggled at the happy task of photographing their churches, I am indebted to Dr. John A. Miles, Jr. of the University of California Press for his encouragement from the inception of this project. And there is, of course, Bing Crosby, Barry Fitzgerald and Pat O'Brien.

This book was made possible by new friends: Buzz and George Erikson of Ross-Erikson Publishers, Inc. of Santa Barbara, who very quickly demonstrated a respect appropriate to the individuals who originally peopled the old missions. And I am especially appreciative of the many gifts of Lois Shearer, my editor, who prior to cutting never failed to anesthetize.

The final reality of the book owes much to Al Madison and the staff of the University Printing Service. Floyd Booth, Owen Hummel, Don Stefonowicz and Lee Meloche are among those who continually prove that fine printing is a celebration.

B.W.B.

Missoula, Montana
September, 1979

Appendix

THE MISSIONS AND THEIR FOUNDERS

1. Mission San Diego de Alcala, Fr. Junipero Serra, O.F.M.
   July 16, 1769.
2. Mission San Carlos Borromeo de Carmelo, Fr. Junipero Serra, O.F.M.
   June 3, 1770.
3. Mission San Antonio de Padua, Fr. Junipero Serra, O.F.M.
   July 14, 1771.
4. Mission San Gabriel Arcangel, Fr. Junipero Serra, O.F.M.
   September 8, 1771.
5. Mission San Luis Obisbo de Tolosa, Fr. Junipero Serra, O.F.M.
   September 1, 1772.
6. Mission San Francisco de Asis, Fr. Francisco Palou, O.F.M.
   October 9, 1776.
7. Mission San Juan Capistrano, Fr. Fermin Lasuen, O.F.M.
   November 1, 1776.
8. Mission Santa Clara de Asis, Fr. Tomas de la Pena, O.F.M.
   January 12, 1777.
9. Mission San Buenaventura, Fr. Junipero Serra, O.F.M.
   March 31, 1782.
10. Mission Santa Barbara, Fr. Fermin Lasuen, O.F.M.
    December 4, 1786.
11. Mission La Purisima Concepcion, Fr. Fermin Lasuen, O.F.M.
    December 8, 1787.
12. Mission Santa Cruz, Fr. Fermin Lasuen, O.F.M.
    September 25, 171.
13. Mission Nuestra Senora de la Soledad, Fr. Fermin Lasuen, O.F.M.
    October 9, 1791.
14. Mission San Jose, Fr. Fermin Lasuen, O.F.M.
    June 11, 1797.
15. Mission San Juan Bautista, Fr. Fermin Lasuen, O.F.M.
    June 24, 1797.
16. Mission San Miguel Arcangel, Fr. Fermin Lasuen, O.F.M.
    July 25, 1797.
17. Mission San Fernando Rey de Espana, Fr. Fermin Lasuen, O.F.M.
    September 8, 1797.
18. Mission San Luis Rey de Francia, Fr. Fermin Lasuen, O.F.M.
    June 13, 1798.
19. Mission Santa Ines, Fr. Estevan Tapis, O.F.M.
    September 17, 1804.
20. Mission San Rafael Arcangel, Fr. Vicente Sarria, O.F.M.
    December 14, 1817.
21. Mission San Francisco de Solano, Fr. Jose Altimira, O.F.M.
    July 4, 1823.

THE FATHER-PRESIDENTS

Fr. Junipero Serra, O.F.M. 1769-1784
Fr. Francisco Palou, O.F.M. 1784-1785
Fr. Fermin Francisco de Lasuen, O.F.M. 1785-1803
Fr. Estevan Tapis, O.F.M. 1803-1812
Fr. Jose Senan, O.F.M. 1812-1815
Fr. Mariano Payeras, O.F.M. 1815-1819
Fr. Jose Senan, O.F.M. 1819-1823
Fr. Vicente Francisco Sarria, O.F.M. 1823-1825
Fr. Narciso Duran, O.F.M. 1825-1827
Fr. Jose Bernardo Sanchez, O.F.M. 1827-1831
Fr. Narciso Duran, O.F.M. 1831-1838
Fr. Jose Joaquin Jimeno, O.F.M. 1838-1844
Fr. Narciso Duran, O.F.M. 1844-1846

PRESIDIO FOUNDINGS

The Presidio of San Diego, July 16, 1769.
The Presidio of Monterey, June 3, 1770.
The Presidio of San Francisco, September 17, 1776.
The Presidio of Santa Barbara, April 2, 1782.

MISSION PUEBLOS FOUNDED

San Luis Obispo, September 1, 1772.
San Juan Capistrano, November 1, 1776.
San Juan Bautista, June 24, 1797.
Sonoma, July 4, 1823.

CIVIL PUEBLOS FOUNDED

San Jose, November 29, 1777.
Los Angeles, September 4, 1781.
Branciforte (now Greater Santa Cruz) 1797.

THE SPANISH GOVERNORS OF CALIFORNIA

Gaspar de Portola, 1768-1770.
Felipe de Barri, 1770-1775. (Alta and Baja)
Pedro Fages (Alta)
Felipe de Neve, 1775-1782.
Pedro Fages, 1782-1791.
Jose Antonio Romeu, 1791-1792.
Jose Joaquin de Arrillaga, 1792-1794.
Diego de Borica, 1794-1800.
Jose Joaquin de Arrillaga, 1800-1814.
Jose Arguello, 1814-1815.
Pablo Vicente Sola, 1815-1822.

THE MEXICAN GOVERNORS OF CALIFORNIA

Luis Arguello, 1822-1825.
Jose Maria de Echeandia, 1825-1831.
Manuel Victoria, 1831-1832.
Pio Pico, 1832.
Jose Maria de Echeandia. (Southern Governor) 1832-1833.
Augustin Vicente Zamorano (Northern Governor) 1832-1833.
Jose Figueroa, 1833-1835.
Jose Castro, 1835-1836.
Nicolas Gutierrez, 1836.
Mariano Chico, 1836.
Nicolas Gutierrez, 1836.
Juan Bautista Alvardo, 1836-1842.
Manuel Micheltorena, 1842-1845.
Pio Pico, 1845-1846.
Jose Maria Flores, 1846-1847.

List of Illustrations

V	Sir Harry Downie
XIV	The Infant Jesus, Mission San Juan Bautista
XVIII	Map of the California Missions
3	A Simple Mission Plan
6	St. Francis of Assissi, Mission San Diego de Alcala
7	Fr. Junipero Serra and Native Child, Mission San Gabriel Arcangel
11	Facsimile of St. Francis Medal
12	Native Cradleboard, San Diego Museum of Man
13	Native Basket, San Diego Museum of Man
21	California Landscape
22	Native Baskets, San Diego Museum of Man
23	Native Dolls, San Diego Museum of Man
32	California Landscape
34	Cottonwood Tree, Mission La Purisima Concepcion
41	Facsimile of Fr. Serra Medal and Signature
42	The Holy Infant of Atocha, Mission San Diego de Alcala
43	Exterior, Mission San Diego de Alcala
48	Interior, Mission San Diego de Alcala
52	Exterior, Mission San Carlos Borromeo de Carmelo
53	Exterior, Mission San Carlos Borromeo de Carmelo
59	California Landscape
60	Device for teaching music, Mission San Antonio de Padua
61	Exterior, Mission San Antonio de Padua
63	Interior, Mission San Antonio de Padua
68	Exterior, Mission San Gabriel Arcangel
69	Exterior, Mission San Gabriel Arcangel
76	Native Tile, Mission La Purisima Concepion
77	Exterior, Mission San Luis Obispo de Tolosa
81	Altar, Mission San Luis Obispo de Tolosa
84	Fragment of Altar lining, Mission San Francisco de Asis
85	Exterior, Mission San Francisco de Asis
92	Iron Cross, Mission San Luis Rey de Francia
94	Our Lady of Sorrows and the Corpus, Mission San Antonio de Padua
99	Mission Bell, Mission San Miguel Arcangel
108	Sanctus Bell, Mission La Purisima Concepcion
109	Exterior, Mission San Juan Capistrano
118	Statue of St. Clare, Mission Santa Clara de Asis
119	Exterior, Mission Santa Clara de Asis
127	Altar Stone, Mission San Jose
128	Crucifix, Mission Santa Barbara
129	Exterior, Mission San Buenaventura
136	Native Pottery, San Diego Museum of Man
137	Exterior, Mission Santa Barbara
141	Interior, Mission Santa Barbara
147	Yellow pitaya — a cactus flower

148 Interior, Statue of La Purisima Concepcion
149 Exterior, Mission La Purisima Concepcion
158 Kitchen, Mission San Luis Rey de Francia
164 Native Basket, San Diego Museum of Man
165 Exterior, Mission Santa Cruz
172 Altar, Our Lady of Solitude
173 Exterior, Mission Nuestra Senora de la Soledad
179 Cylindropuntia — a cactus
180 Interior, Mission San Jose
181 Exterior, Mission San Jose
190 Hand-crank organ: Mission San Juan Bautista
191 Exterior, Mission San Juan Bautista
199 Interior, Mission San Juan Bautista
202 Exterior, Mission San Miguel Arcangel
203 Exterior, Mission San Miguel Arcangel
207 Interior, Mission San Miguel Arcangel
214 Oven, Mission San Miguel Arcangel
218 Cholla, Mission San Miguel Arcangel
220 Violin of native manufacture, Mission Santa Barbara
229 Twelfth Station of the Cross, Mission San Jose
230 Mateo, Marcos, Lucas and Juan, Mission San Fernando Rey de Espana
231 Exterior, Mission San Fernando Rey de Espana
241 Illuminated book, Mission San Miguel Arcangel
242 Bells from Museum Collection, Mission San Luis Rey de Francia
243 Exterior, Mission San Luis Rey de Francia
249 Interior, Mission San Luis Rey de Francia
254 Campanile, Asistencia San Antonio de Pala
256 Prickly pear cactus
257 Exterior, Mission Santa Ines
264 Native basket, San Diego Museum of Man
265 Exterior, Mission San Rafael Arcangel
276 Votive candles, Mission San Diego de Alcala
277 Exterior, Mission San Francisco de Solano
287 Holy Virgin and Child, Mission La Purisima Concepcion
288 Ruined adobe wall, Mission Soledad
289 Scare crow, Mission La Purisima Concepcion
295 Tree, Mission San Juan Bautista
296 El Camino Real Marker, Mission San Diego de Alcala
297 Cross, Mission San Antonio de Padua
303 Milagros, Mission San Juan Bautista

Selected Bibliography and Additional Readings

Bancroft, Hubert Howe. *California Pastoral, 1769-1848.* San Francisco: The History Company, 1888.

———. *History of California,* Vols. I, II and III. San Francisco: The History Company, Publishers, 1886.

Berger, John A. *The Franciscan Missions of California.* New York: G. P. Putnam's Sons, 1941.

Bolton, Herbert Eugene. *Anza's California Expeditions,* 5 vols. Berkeley, Calif.: University of California Press, 1930.

———. *Fray Juan Crespi, Missionary Explorer on the Pacific Coast 1769-1774.* Berkeley, Calif.: University of California Press, 1927.

———. *Outpost of Empire: The Story of the Founding of San Francisco.* New York: Alfred A. Knopf, 1931.

———. *Palou's Historical Memoirs of New California,* 4 vols. Berkeley, Calif.: University of California Press, 1926.

———. *The Spanish Borderlands.* New Haven: Yale University Press, 1921.

Chapman, Charles E. *A History of California: The Spanish Period.* New York: The Macmillan Company, 1921.

Cook, Sherburne Friend. *The Conflict Between the California Indian and White Civilization.* Berkeley and Los Angeles, Calif.: University of California Press, 1943.

Corle, Edwin. *The Royal Highway.* Indianapolis, Ind.: The Bobbs-Merrill Co., Inc., 1949.

Correia, Delia Richards. *Lasuen in California.* Berkeley, Calif.: University of California Press, 1934.

Culleton, James. *Indians and Pioneers of Old Monterey.* Fresno, Calif.: Academy of California Church History, 1950.

Dana, Richard Henry, Jr. *Two Years Before the Mast: A Personal Narrative.* Boston and New York: Houghton Mifflin Company, 1884.

Da Silva, Owen Francis, ed. *Mission Music of California.* Los Angeles, Calif.: W. F. Lewis, 1941.

Davis, William Heath. *Seventy-Five Years in California — A History of Events and Life in California: Personal, Political and Military.* San Francisco: John Howell, 1929.

Dutton, Davis, ed. *Missions of California.* New York: Westways Magazine, Ballantine Books, 1972.

Elder, David Paul. *The Old Spanish Missions of California.* San Francisco: Paul Elder and Company, 1913.

Engelhardt, Rev. Zephyrin, O.F.M., *The Franciscans in California.* Harbor Springs, Michigan: Holy Childhood Indian School, 1897.

———. *The Holy Man of Santa Clara: or Life, Virtues and Miracles of Fr. Magin Catala, O.F.M.* San Francisco: The James H. Barry Company, 1909.

_____. *The Missions and Missionaries of California.* San Francisco: The James H. Barry Company, 1916.

_____. Individual Missions: *San Antonio de Padua,* 1929; *San Buenaventura,* 1930; *San Diego,* 1920; *San Fernando Rey,* 1927; *San Francisco,* 1924; *San Gabriel,* 1927; *San Juan Bautista,* 1931; *San Juan Capistrano,* 1922; *San Luis Rey,* 1921; *San Miguel Arcangel,* 1929; *Santa Barbara,* 1923.

Geary, Gerald Joseph. *The Secularization of the California Mission (1810-1846).* Washington, D.C.: Catholic University of America, 1934.

Geiger, Fr. Maynard, O.F.M. *The Life and Times of Fray Junipero Serra,* 2 vols. Washington, D.C.: Academy of American Franciscan History, 1959.

_____. ed. and trans. *Palou's Life of Fray Junipero Serra.* Washington, D.C.: Academy of American Franciscan History, 1955.

_____. *A Pictorial History of the Physical Development of Mission Santa Barbara from Brush Hut to Institutional Greatness, 1786-1963.* San Francisco: The Franciscan Fathers, 1963.

Hawthorne, Hildegarde. *California's Missions, Their Romance and Beauty.* New York: D. Appleton-Century Co., Inc., 1942.

Heizer, R. F. and Whipple, M. A. *The California Indians, A Source Book.* Berkeley, Los Angeles, London; University of California Press, 1971.

Jackson, Helen Hunt. *Father Junipero and the Mission Indians of California.* Boston: Little, Brown & Co., 1902.

_____. *Glimpses of California and the Missions.* Boston: Little, Brown & Co., 1902.

_____. *Ramona.* Boston: Little, Brown & Co., 1939.

James, George Wharton. *In and Out of the Old Missions of California; An Historical and Pictorial Account of the Franciscan Missions.* Boston: Little, Brown and Co., 1905.

_____. *Old Missions and Mission Indians of California.* Los Angeles, Calif.: B. R. Baumgardt, 1895.

_____. *Picturesque Pala, The Story of the Mission Chapel of San Antonio de Pala.* Pasadena, Calif.: George Wharton James, 1916.

Johnson, Paul C. et al, ed. *The California Missions: A Pictorial History.* Menlo Park, Calif.: Lane Book Company, 1964.

King, Kenneth Moffat. *Mission to Paradise: The Story of Junipero Serra and the Missions of California.* Chicago: Franciscan Herald Press, 1956.

Kroeber, Alfred, Louis. *Handbook of the Indians of California.* Berkeley: California Book Company, Ltd., 1953.

_____. *A Mission Record of the California Indians.* Berkeley: University of California Press, 1908.

Lummis, Charles Fletcher. *The Spanish Pioneers and the California Missions.* Chicago: A. C. McClurg & Co., 1929.

Newcomb, Rexford. *The Old Mission Churches and Historic Houses of California.* Philadelphia: J. B. Lippincott Co., 1925, 1953.

Older, Cora Miranda. *California Missions and Their Romances.* New York: Coward-McCann, 1938.

Palou, Francisco. *The Founding of the First California Missions.* San Francisco: Nueva California Press, 1934.

_____ *Life of Fray Junipero Serra*, trans. and annotated by Fr. Maynard Geiger, O.F.M. Washington, D.C.: Academy of American Franciscan History, 1955.

Priestley, Herbert Ingram. *Franciscan Explorations in California*. Glendale, Calif.: Arthur H. Clark Co., 1946.

_____ *Pedro Fages*. Berkeley, Calif.: University of California Press, 1937.

Repplier, Agnes. *Junipero Serra, Pioneer Colonist of California*. Garden City, N.Y.: Doubleday, Doran and Co., Inc., 1947.

Richman, Irving Berdine. *California Under Spain and Mexico 1535-1847*. New York: Houghton Mifflin Co., 1911.

Sanchez, Nellie Van de Grift. *Spanish Aracadia*. Los Angeles, Calif.: Powell Publishing Co., 1929.

Saunders, Charles Francis. *The California Padres and Their Missions*. New York: Houghton Mifflin Co., 1915.

_____ *Capistrano Nights; Tales of California Mission Town*. New York: R. M. McBride & Co., 1930.

Smith, Frances Rand. *The Architectural History of Mission San Carlos Borromeo*. Berkeley, Calif.: Historical Survey Commission, 1921.

_____ *The Mission of San Antonio de Padua*. Stanford, Calif.: Stanford University Press, 1932.

Spearman, Arthur Dunning, S. J. *The Five Franciscan Churches of Mission Santa Clara*. Palo Alto, Calif.: The National Press, 1963.

Stern, Aloysius S., S. J. *Magin Catala, O.F.M.: The Holy Man of Santa Clara*. San Francisco: Privately printed.

Tibesar, Antonine, ed. *Writings of Junipero Serra*, 3 vols. Washington, D.C.: Academy of American Franciscan History, 1955.

Index of People and Places

A

Achois Comihavit, 236
Aqueda, 62
Alameda, 150
Alejo, 245
Altimira, Jose, Father, 279, 280, 281
Amadis, 20
Ambris, Doroteo, Father, 292
Amurrio, Gregorio, Father, 109, 110, 111
Anza, Juan Bautista de, 86, 87
Aquinas, Thomas Saint, 130
Arguello, Alferez, 115
Arguello, Concepcion, 246, 271
Arguello, Luis Antonio, 270, 271, 272, 280
Arrillaga, Joaquin de, Governor, 176, 238, 240, 247
Arroyo, Father, 196
Assisi, Asisi, 8, 9, 10
Avila, Jose, Maria, 274
Ayala, Don Juan Manuel de, 86

B

Bacon, Roger, 8
Balageur, Spain, 57
Barcenilla, Isidoro, Father, 184
Bodega Bay, 245
Borica, Diego, Governor, 195, 238, 240
Bouchard, Hyppolite de, 56, 57, 114, 115, 140, 142, 170
Branciforte, 167, 168, 169, 170, 171, 181, 233
Butron, Manuel, 187

C

Caballer, Jose Prior, Father, 79, 80
Cabot, Juan, Father, 208, 209
Cabrillo, Juan Rodriguez, 15, 16, 24
Califa, 20
Cambou, Pedro Benito, Father, 70
Camero, Manuel, 232
Carpenteria, 16, 273
Carrillo, Carlas, 259
Catala, Magin de, Father, 123
Catalonia, Spain, 243

Channel — Cueva

Channel Islands, 16
Chavez, (artist), 196
Cipriano, 185
Clement X, Pope, 284
Columbus, Christopher, 14
Cordoba, Alberto de, 167
Cortez, Hernando, 14, 15
Coyote, 4, 29, 30, 74, 75, 90, 91, 105, 106, 107, 216, 217, 226, 227, 228
Crespi, Juan, Father, 35, 36, 42, 194, 299
Cueva, Pedro de la, Father, 184

D

Dana, Richard Henry, Jr., 271
Diego, Juan, 197, 198
Doak, Thomas, (artist), 196
Dodson, Benjamen, 200
Dominguez, Juan Jose, 235
Downie, Harry, Sir, 155, 201, 297, 300, 301, 302, 304
Downieville, California, 300
Drummond, 194
Dumetz, Francisco, 130

E

Echeandia, Jose Marie de, Governor, 272, 273, 275
Encino Ranch, 236
Esplandian, 20
Estanisloa (Stanislaus), Chief, 186, 187

F

Fages, Pedro, Captain, Governor, 194, 238, 239
Farrell, Lawrence, Father, 201, 301
Ferdinand, King, 78
Figueroa, Jose, Governor, 275, 283, 285, 289, 290
Fitch, Henry Delano, 272
"Flower," (Mrs. Moses Grosz), 169
Fort Ross, 247, 248, 282
Francis; see St. Francis
Fremont, John C., 291
Fuster, Vincente, Father, 51

318

G

Geiger, Maynard, Father, 302
Golden Gate, 86
Gomez, Francisco, Father, 36
Grajera, Captain, 244
Grosz, Moses, 168, 169, 170
Great Britian, 39
Guadalupe-Hidalgo, 198

H

Haraszthy, Agoston, 194
Horra, Antonio de la Concepcion, Father, 204, 210

I

Ibanez, Florencio, Father, 176, 240
Iturbide, Augustin, Col., 269

J

Jackson, Helen Hunt, 80, 155
Jayme, Luis, Father, 51, 111
Joseph (San Jose), 49, 117, 140, 183

K

Krug, Charles, 194
Kuskov, Ivan, 246

L

La Brea, 235
La Purisima, (Mary), 49, 55, 67, 70, 71, 88, 140, 148, 151, 248
La Purisima Concepcion, Mission, 129, 148, 149, 150, 151, 152, 153, 154, 155, 156, 197, 237, 262, 263, 292, 302
Larra, Jose de, 232, 235
Lasuen, Fermin Francisco de, Father-President, 109, 110, 111, 137, 138, 151, 165, 174, 175, 183, 195, 203, 204, 236, 238, 239, 299
Lompoc, California, 155
Los Angeles, California, 129, 150, 167, 181, 231, 232, 233, 234, 235, 236, 274, 275, 302
Los Robles, 62

M

Maljalapu, 257, 258
Mallorca, 39
Maria, Juana, 143, 144, 145, 146

Marin, 269
Martiarena, Jose, Father, 195
Martinez, Luis Antonio, Father, 80, 82, 83
Mary, see: La Purisima
Mateo, 245
Mesa, Antonio, 232, 234, 235
Mexico City, 14, 16, 18
Monterey, 16, 45, 53, 55, 57, 58, 78, 82, 87, 194, 204, 269, 270, 274
Moraga, Comisionado, 167
Moreno, Filipe, 82, 83
Moreno, Jose, 232, 234
Mugartegui, Pablo, Father, 111
Munras, Esteban, 206

Mc

McEldowney, Mabel, 301

N

Nanaguani, 267
Navarro, Jose, 232, 235
Neve, Felipe de, Governor, 130, 181, 231, 232, 234, 238, 239
New Helvetica, 248
Nidiver, George, (Mr. and Mrs.), 145, 146
Niebaum, Gustave, 194
Nuestra Senora de la Soledad, Mission, 173, 174, 175, 176, 177, 178, 183, 239, 240, 294, 302

O

Ojai, 133
Ortega, Jose, Francisco de, Sergeant, 85
O'Sullivan, St. John, Father, 299, 300, 301
Our Lady of Angels, 232
Our Lady of Guadalupe, 197, 215
Our Lady of Refuge, 262
Our Lady of Solitude, 172, 175
Our Lady of Sorrows, 87, 88, 94

P

Pacheco, Romualdo, Captain, 274
Padres, Jose Maria, 284, 285
Padilla, J. C. (artist), 198
Palou, Francisco, Father, 80, 88, 120
Palma, 39

Parrow, Fernando, Father, 36, 40
Paso Robles, 204, 211, 212
Payeras, Mariano, Father, 267, 281
Pedragoso, El, 138
Perez, Eubalia, 73
Petaluma, 283
Petra, 39
Peyri, Antonio, Father, 243, 244, 245, 248, 255
Pico, Pio, 275
Pieras, Miguel, Father, 62
Poinsett, Joel Roberts, 191, 192
Point Conception, 16
Point Loma, 15
Pomponio, 269
Popeloutechoni, 194
Portola, Don Gaspar de, Captain, Governor, 18, 35, 45, 46, 53, 54, 55, 57, 58, 238
Pratt, Pedro, Dr., 37
Puebla, 57

Q

Quentin, 269
Quintero, Luis, 232, 234, 235

R

Reed, William, 210, 211
Reyes, Francisco, Alcalde, 236
Rezanov, Nikolai Petrovich, 246, 271
Rivera, y Moncado Fernando, Captain, Governor, 233, 238, 239
Rodriguez, Amancio, Monsignor, 200
Rodriguez, Pablo, 232
Romeu, Jose Antonio, Governor, 239
Rosas, Alejandro, 232
Rosas, Bastillo, 232, 234
Ruiz, Manuel, 56

S

Sacramento, 248
Sal, Don Hermenegildo, 165, 166
Salinas River, 61
San Antonio de Padua, Mission, 61, 62, 63, 64, 65, 66, 67, 211, 292, 299, 302
San Antonio de Pala, Mission Asistencia, 125, 178, 252, 253
San Buenaventura, Mission, 129, 130, 131, 132, 133, 134, 135, 294

San Carlos Borromeo de Carmelo, Mission, 52, 53, 54, 55, 56, 57, 61, 78, 135, 166, 178, 292, 299, 300, 301
San Damiano, 9
San Diego, 2, 15, 35, 36, 40, 44, 45, 46, 47, 49, 53, 55, 66, 70, 78, 79, 86, 109, 110, 111, 114, 150, 194, 243, 244, 261, 272, 274, 281, 289, 293, 302, 304
San Diego de Alcala, Mission, 44, 45, 46, 47, 49, 50, 66, 86, 109, 110, 111, 112, 114, 130, 293, 297, 298
San Fernando College, 244
San Fernando Rey de Espana, Mission, 231, 232, 233, 234, 235, 236, 237, 238, 239, 240, 241, 291
San Fernando Valley, 236
San Francisco de Asis, Mission, 85, 86, 87, 88, 89, 150, 166, 169, 183, 185, 265, 267, 279, 280, 281, 282, 300, 301, 302
San Francisco de Solano, Mission, 277, 278, 279, 280, 281, 282, 283, 284, 285, 286, 294, 302
San Gabriel Arcangel, Mission, 68, 69, 70, 71, 72, 73, 75, 109, 110, 130, 152, 232, 233, 292
San Jose, Mission, 181, 182, 183, 184, 185, 186, 187, 188, 240, 282, 294
San Jose de Guadalupe, 181, 182, 183, 185, 186, 187, 188, 233
San Juan Bautista, Mission, 191, 192, 193, 194, 195, 196, 197, 198, 199, 200, 201, 240, 293, 302
San Juan Capistrano, Mission, 109, 110, 111, 112, 113, 114, 115, 116, 117, 248, 290, 299
San Luis Obispo de Tolosa, Mission, 77, 78, 79, 80, 81, 82, 83, 149, 292, 302
San Luis Rey de Francia, Mission, 66, 184, 240, 243, 244, 245, 246, 247, 248, 249, 250, 251, 252, 253, 254, 255, 290, 298
San Mateo, 150
San Miguel Arcangel, Mission, 69, 203, 204, 205, 206, 207, 208, 209, 210, 211, 212, 213, 214, 215, 240, 291, 292
San Nicholas Isle, 142, 143, 144, 145
San Pedro, 15, 235
San Rafael Arcangel, Mission, 69, 165,

266, 267, 268, 269, 270, 271, 272, 273, 274, 275, 280, 281, 282, 291

San Simeon, 211, 212

Santa Ana, 133

Santa Barbara, 210, 233, 236, 259, 260, 263, 272

Santa Barbara, Mission, 82, 129, 137, 138, 139, 140, 141, 142, 143, 144, 145, 146, 149, 150, 299

Santa Clara, St. Clare, 118, 119, 120

Santa Clara de Asis, Mission, 119, 120, 121, 122, 123, 124, 125, 126, 166, 222, 294, 299

Santa Cruz, Mission, 165, 166, 167, 168, 169, 170, 171, 183, 239

Santa Ines, Mission, 152, 240, 257, 258, 259, 260, 261, 262, 263, 293

Santa Lucia Mountains, 61

Santa Monica, 15

Santa Rosa, 283, 284

Santiago, Juan Norberto de, Father, 244

Santia Maria, Vincente de, Father, 130

San Vincente, Augustin Fernandes de, 270

Sarria, Vincente Francisco de, Father-President, 177, 178, 281, 294

Scher, Philip, Father (Bishop) 301

Scotus, Duns, 8

Senan, Jose, Father-President, 281

Serra, Junipero, Father-President, 18, 35, 36, 37, 39, 40, 43, 44, 45, 49, 51, 53, 54, 55, 56, 61, 62, 64, 70, 77, 78, 79, 85, 95, 111, 112, 121, 129, 130, 135, 137, 138, 166, 193, 209, 238, 239, 243, 281, 298, 299, 300, 302, 304

Sinova, Jose Francisco, 235

Sitjar, Buenaventura, Father, 62, 66, 203, 204, 210

Solorzano, Dona Ascencion, 201

Sola, Pablo Vicente, Governor, 240, 247, 269

Somera, Angel, Father, 70, 71

Sonoma, 2, 78, 282, 302

St. Bonaventure, 8

St. Dominic, 140, 196

St. Francis, 8, 9, 10, 13, 16, 85, 86, 87, 88, 119, 120, 140, 183, 195, 196, 222, 232, 246, 281, 282

St. Gregory, 222

St. Isadore, 196

St. Pascal Baylon, 196

Sugert, 166

Sumtache, 208

Sutter, Johann, 248, 282, 283

T

Taboada, Gil y, Father, 267

Tapis, Estavan, Father-President, 201, 259

Taylor, B. M., 200

Tixlina, 78

U

Umpqua, 212

Ursulino, 51

V

Vallejo, M. G., 186, 283, 291

Vandalia, (Momma), 251

Vanegas, Jose, 232, 234

Vargas, Manuel, 261

Vatica, 203

Ventura, 15, 134, 135, 150

Victoria, Manuel, Governor, 273, 274

Vignes, Jean Luis, 193

Villavicencio, Felix, 232

Viscaino, Juan, Father, 36, 40

W

Wolfskill, William, 193

Z

Zacatula, 14

Zucu, 130, 131

Zumarraga, Bishop, 197